furred and feathered
WILD GAME
from bullet to table

A comprehensive and
environmentally friendly
guide for handling and
preparing the world's
finest meats

Jack McCready

Published by:
WorldComm®
a division of Creativity, Inc.

Publisher: Ralph Roberts
Executive Editor: Kathryn L. Hall
Production Manager: Carey E. Watson

Editor: Tammy Jones

Cover Design: WorldComm®
Interior Design and Electronic Page Assembly: WorldComm®

Indexing: The Roberts Group, Greensboro, NC

©First Edition O.T. Powell, Owner, The Powell Company 1973
©Second Edition O.T. Powell, Owner, The Powell Company 1993

Reproduction and translation of any part of this work beyond that permitted by Sections 107 and 108 of the United States Copyright Act without permission of the copyright owner is unlawful.

Printed in the United States of America.

10 9 8 7 6 5 4 3 2 1

ISBN 1-56664-031-8

Library of Congress: 93-060865

The author and publisher have made every effort in the preparation of this book to ensure the accuracy of the information. However, the information in this book is sold without warranty, either express or implied. Neither the author nor WorldComm Press will be liable for any damages caused or alleged to be caused directly, indirectly, incidentally, or consequentially by the information in this book.

Names of products mentioned in this book known to be or suspected of being trademarks or service marks are capitalized. Use of a product or service mark in this book should not be regarded as affecting the validity of any trademark or service mark.

The opinions expressed in this book are solely those of the author and are not necessarily those of WorldComm Press.

WorldComm Press—a Division of Creativity, Inc., 65 Macedonia Road, Alexander, North Carolina 28701, (704) 252-9515—is a full service publisher.

Contents

A Foreword
From the Publisher

Many people generously contributed to this book. Hunters with proven expertise, wildlife agents, naturalists, nutritionists, state university researchers, and game commissions in various parts of the United States cooperated in the gathering of information. These sources made the present work possible and to them we offer a sincere expression of gratitude.

Supervising, collating and condensing the masses of research, Jack McCready expressed it all in his very readable style. His byline has appeared on everything from books to specialized articles in national magazines. An outdoorsman who grew up in a family with a long and strong hunting tradition, McCready was bagging his first small game around the age of twelve with a secondhand twenty-two. Editors of several leading men's magazines know him as a writer with a rare talent for both research and words. In the present instance, his talent has produced a fine work which can be read for fun or if studied with the same diligence required by any textbook, it offers a unique education.

The sport of hunting is greater than ever and rapidly increasing in popularity. Dedicated conservationists in public service have restored, sometimes miraculously, wild game varieties that were once threatened with extinction. As a result, among modern and urbanized nations, the United States today is a hunter's paradise, with an annual game kill soaring into the hundreds of millions of pounds. But if conservationists have come a long way in restoring a national asset, very few of us know how to get the most from it. Authorities estimate that seventy percent of the game meat kill is wasted in the field and in garbage cans at home. Most of the remainder reaches the kitchen in a state of abuse, its potentials for cooking and eating depleted. The dollar waste is shameful and the hunter rarely experiences the full rewards of the sport.

"What do I do now?" Asked over a fresh kill, this question will usually receive contradictory pet theories and biased opinions from different hunters. While methods that vary in minor detail may work equally well in handling a kill, there are basic rules grounded in scientific facts that are vital to the welfare of the meat. This book reflects a comprehensive effort to present the best of proven guidelines for handling the game kills commonly hunted in the United States. Nothing substitutes for that greatest of teachers, experience. But nothing is worse than repeated mis-experience, and here for perhaps the first time the new hunter will find a foundation for proper experience and the more seasoned hunter may discover reasons to review—and perhaps revise—some long-held habits. The blood-and-guts job posed by a freshly killed carcass is for less than nothing if the hunter only guesses at what must be done.

1 The Three Hunters

Any marksman can kill game. But killing is merely a part of the hunting experience, perhaps the easiest. It's the difficulties between kill and kitchen that separate the shooter from the hunter.

1 | *The Three Hunters*

Ore day three men, Zeke, Albert, and Horace, went out to hunt. They were strangers, and they hunted in locations miles apart. Each man killed a deer. The animals and circumstances of each hunter were almost identical, and each man went his way without ever laying eyes on the others. That's all there is to the story, except for the most important detail: Each hunter handled his kill differently, and only one brought home a prime selection of meat.

Any marksman can kill game. But killing is merely a part of the hunting experience, perhaps the easiest. It's the difficulties between kill and kitchen that separate the shooter from the hunter. The truly proficient hunter knows that the quality of the meat on the table depends on the treatment afforded it from the very moment of the kill. The finest chef can't undo damage wreaked by sloppy field handling.

Good field handling has its problems in the best of circumstances. When the weather is bitter and the terrain forbidding, the kill-to-kitchen phase may offer obstacles not encountered in any other sport. In the total action of hunting there's little room for a weak stomach or wavering determination.

Take our friend, Zeke. Despite the backwoodsy flavor of

his name, Zeke, like most of us, is more accustomed to tall buildings than towering trees. His concept of hunting is glamorous and exciting. He's attracted to the thought of rugged country, stalking the game, and pulling off the perfect shot. That's all there is to it. He learned to be a crack shot in the army. He's so eager to get started that he hardly sleeps the night before he treks off.

Zeke bought a hunting license and finished off the preliminaries at a sporting goods store where he bought ammo and clothing. The clerk, who had never hunted anything gamier than blondes, told Zeke all about hunting, backing up the advice with a few touch-the-surface pamphlets and a chart which showed where to plug various animals for the cleanest kill.

Zeke heads off for the woods, and his luck is good. His aim is perfect, and before the bird life can settle down from the crash of the gun, Zeke, with quickened breath and slightly glazed eyes, is excitedly running up to the fallen deer. As he pauses and looks at the dead buck, Zeke begins to have second thoughts. Somehow the reality of this moment hadn't got through to him when he was slouched comfortably on the sofa at home, thumbing through a hunting magazine with a cold beer at his elbow.

He looks at the glistening hide and his mind begins to picture the hot blood and steaming guts beneath. He thinks of dismembering all of that bloody bulk. Finally, a flash of inspiration lifts his spirits. He'll just haul the carcass home as is, hang it in the garage, and turn the problem over to George, one of his friends. George cut up a deer of his own a couple years ago. Of course, it may be two or three days before George can do the favor. But the weather's cool enough to keep the meat from rotting, and a little delay can't make that much difference...

Separated from Zeke by umpteen imaginary miles, Albert is at the same moment standing over his kill. Unlike Zeke, Albert has spent a good part of his leisure life in the woods. Brother, he really knows the score. He's killed his own share of deer and will tell you everything there is to know about hunting every chance he gets. His head is so full of mis-experience, opinions, advice from other hunters of his own breed that there isn't room for another grain. As coolly confident as the scientist of yesteryear who could prove the earth was flat, Albert steps right up and reaches for his skinning knife. And when Albert in due time hosted his venison dinner, his friends braced with pre-dinner drinks for another of Albert's offerings.

Which brings us to Horace, whose story you've probably already guessed. He's an average family man, commuting to his job five days a week. A modest sort, he won't be heard spouting off like Albert. But in field and wood, he's the man to imitate. Like all good hunters, Horace has a naturalist's eye for the outdoors. He likes the smell of a sage field and the rustle of frosty leaves. He's interested in wild creatures, their habits and habitats, and he knows their value.

Many hunters, Horace observed, share a trait with average weekend golfers. They never come to grips with the self-disciplined practices necessary to peak proficiency. Professionalism is the key to the right state of mind and conduct in any amateur sport. The golfer hacks away, trying to build a game on pet theories, trial and error, and the misbegotten tips offered by well meaning friends. Likewise the hunter takes the same faulty habits into the field season after season. The situations are more disconcerting and frustrating than satisfactory. And there's no valid reason why they should be.

Viewed properly, hunting is an action that begins with the loading of a gun and ends with the loading of a succulent dinner plate. The hunter who doesn't score in the total action cheats himself of a rare personal experience. A quirk in the hunting mentality may be at fault. The tendency is always present to feel that the contest is over when the animal is dead. Everything after the kill is anti-climatic. But the meat is a long way from the dinner table, and the hunter couldn't pick a worse time to let down.

Well now, Albert didn't let down. He went right into action, guided by a lot of wrong notions and mis-experience. He put meat on the table, ate it and thought it tasted all right, with its usual gamy, musty, and slightly high tang. His friends politely agreed that the dinner had been unusual eating. Truth is, neither Albert nor his friends had ever tasted game meat at its average goodness, much less its best. They had no yardstick whatsoever for comparison. A piece of beef handled like Albert's venison would have turned the dogs away. The fact that Albert's offering was at all edible is proof of game's inherent excellence. Game forages, exercises, and expends body wastes as nature intended, resulting in a low-fat, nutritious product that kept our forebears as leanly tough as the frontier.

But let's leave the queasy stomachs of Albert and his friends at the dinner table and get back to Horace the Hunter. As a novice talking with other hunters, Horace had the early suspicion that far too many gun-carriers were apt to foul up from the moment of the kill onward. Many had never really stressed in their own minds the problems of field treatment. They went equipped to kill but without fundamental knowledge for the aftermath. His friends tossed contradictory ideas at Horace, one hunter's pet theory being shrugged off as unimportant by another. It was all very confusing. If all of the conflicting advice was correct, then field treatment of the kill lost its urgency. Most any measures would do. Horace couldn't buy such a slipshod conclusion. True, minor variations in field treatment might not affect the outcome. Sometimes conditions of terrain, weather, and size of the kill force the hunter to improvise. Successful improvisation is one of the pleasures of hunting. But there had to be, Horace reasoned, certain basics in field treatment that couldn't be violated without damaging the meat.

Horace began his education with a common-sense approach. He studied material from his state wildlife department and the extension division of his state university. In a pleasant hour of reading he would soak up the results of perhaps weeks of studies by a team of experts. He went on his early hunts in the company of hunters of proven professionalism, accepting the role of tenderfoot and keeping his eyes and ears open. He bought a few books on the anatomy of wild animals and one on taxidermy. They provided first-step briefings for the ordeal of butchering the meat and delivery of good trophies to the taxidermist.

At first, Horace's wife reacted to his new hobby with a sideward look and crinkled nose. To her, the natural state of meat was in a package from the supermarket. But her doubts dissolved when Horace began bringing home prime condition meat and she discovered the charm of wild game cookery. Nowadays, the neighbors anticipate those dinner invitations, and her wild game hors d'oeuvres and fondues transform informal visits into memorable occasions. And she's delighted by the effect on the household budget when Horace returns from a hunt and loads the freezer.

2 Old Saws with Sharp Teeth

Professionalism in preparation is geared to the type of game, the terrain, and the weather. The objective is always the same: Cool the meat. Keep it cool and clean.

2 | Old Saws With Sharp Teeth

Fellows like Albert have heard the old saws time and again, the very first don't's and do's in the field. They bore him. He knows the score, and he's impatient to get on with some man-sized hunting.

Take the time he killed a buck and had to drag it out of the woods. A covering for the antlers wasn't handy, and it was too much of a drag to go and fetch one. Anyhow, Albert figured, he didn't have very far to move the deer. He looped a quarter-inch rope at the base of the antlers, picked up the free end, stretched out, and started pulling. He hadn't dragged the buck very far when another hunter glimpsed the moving antlers through a break in a thicket.

It happened that this second hunter was hardly a Horace. In fact, he was a character similar to Albert. The antlers had quickly slipped from sight, but he knew that a deer was in the brush dead ahead, and that was enough for him. Well, the first thirty-ought-six slug blasted a miniature foxhole near Albert's feet. The second nipped his sleeve. He imagined it had jerked his arm off. If previously he'd been a shade immune to full respect for gunpowder, he wasn't now.

With a bleat a big mountain billy goat might have envied, Albert dropped everything and took a long dive behind a big oak tree. Thus sheltered, he started hollering and cussing while the sweat popped out in twenty degree weather. Of course, when Albert finally got around to telling the story in the neighborhood tavern, the details had changed considerably. By that time, even in his own mind, Albert was no longer a damn fool damn lucky to be able to talk about it.

The experience almost convinced Albert for a while that there are right and wrong ways of doing things. Game laws, for example, aren't really made up just to complicate the hunter's life, as much as it may seem that way at times. Without the body of law there would be no body of game and the warden or ranger is never unhappier than when he is forced to drive a point home.

Grandpa didn't have to worry with some of the nitpicking details that are so necessary today. No matter how much he shot, more was out there. Grandpa didn't have to fret about the quality of his drinking water, either. Those were the good old days. If his well was pure, he thrived. If contaminated, he died of typhoid. Nice and simple. Grandpa didn't have to contend with rangers, health inspectors, ecologists, and dentists who could save his teeth.

Learning both the letter and spirit of the law is a fairly sound basic with which to start off. The hunter shells out taxes that help foot the bill for the typist in the state wildlife department, the ranger in the field, the clerk in the legislature voting passage of the game law. The hunter gets his money's worth only when he becomes involved and part of the action. State regulations have something to say about the way a kill is handled. So do your homework.

Complementing legal requirements are the kill-to-kitchen rules. Our friend Horace bases his field conduct on a simple axiom: **The Carcass Deserves Slaughterhouse Respect.**

While field conditions rarely duplicate those of the abattoir, the stringent methods associated with the slaughterhouse should never be far from the hunter's mind. Some situations will test his energy, tenacity, and ingenuity to the outer limits. In the field, as in the slaughterhouse, the welfare of the carcass comes first.

Field treatment depends on preparation. Tons of fine meat are ruined because foresight was lacking. Sometimes the novice doesn't know how to prepare adequately, or he's careless in preparation because he subconsciously doubts his "luck."

Always expect the bag limit—and the worst of field situations. Hindsight and self-recrimination unfortunately won't freshen tainted meat.

Professionalism in preparation is geared to the type of game, the terrain, and the weather. The objective is always the same: Cool the meat. Keep it cool and clean. Tainting elements are present the instant the animal dies. The quicker the meat loses its body heat, the better it will taste.

Problems of terrain and weather grow in proportion to the size of the game. Birds and little animals can be dressed and carried in the roughest country. If warm weather is a threat, portable refrigeration in station wagon, car, or at the camp-site will keep small, dressed carcasses tastefully fresh.

The hunter who is going after bigger game must resolve the terrain-weather questions before he takes the field. How rough is the country? How will the kill be transported? Big animals frequently die in spots cussedly contrary to the convenience of the hunter.

How about protection against insects and predators? The weather forecast looks good, encouragingly cold. But what if a southern air mass tricks the weatherman? Are plans made for the welfare of the carcass?

In temperatures of forty degrees or higher, there is no perfect substitute for prompt dressing and refrigeration. Where state law permits, a commercial plant or country storekeeper near the hunting site usually will make a deal for temporary use of cooler space. Or a farmer may have facilities that can be of help for a few dollars.

If a week's hunt is planned, the weather breaks warm, and a deer is dropped in the first hour, pick up the rental option on the cooler space. If two or more hunters have made the trip, draw straws and let the loser be on his way with the carcass. Peace of mind about the condition of the meat will reward the interruption. When the field problems have been licked, the meat must be hauled home.

The hunter driving along with a fine deer lashed across the front fender of his car offers an impressive sight. A worse location for the load could hardly be imagined. After soaking up engine heat for a few miles, a steak cut and cooked from the carcass will certainly reinforce the idea that venison is a gamy, musty meat.

Plans for hauling the larger carcass, either whole or quartered, must follow a few simple rules: locate the meat as far as possible from engine heat; provide for the circulation of cooling air around the meat; don't expose the carcass to bright, direct sunlight even if the air temperature is relatively low.

On an overcast and cool day (below forty degrees) haul the carcass on the top carrier of a car or station wagon, or lashed firmly across the top of a car trunk. If the day is sunny, the interior of a station wagon is fine, if air circulates through open windows. The inside of a car trunk will do, but the lid must not be closed and the sealed-in carcass deprived of air circulation. The lid should be propped open with a stick and secured with a rope or cord.

If the hunter has been in the area several times and knows the local people, the temptation is strong to stop at various pubs on the way home, show off the kill, and buy the drinks.

Pass up the pleasure. Take a couple of snapshots to show around later. The best tasting wild game meat isn't aged outside ye friendly tavern.

3 *Antlered Animals*

True, no hunter can make every shot perfect; but there's little excuse for not trying. The animal best killed for the table is the one that never knew what hit it.

3 | Antlered Animals

Venison has been called the king of meat, and the meat of kings. It remained for us moderns to sell it short, weaned as we are to the pre-packaged, hormone-injected cuts of beef and pork.

Our ancestors knew better. It was a cause for celebration in Sherwood Forest when Robin Hood and his men brought in one of the king's deer. But who has ever heard of those doughty yeomen risking their necks for the king's shoat or heifer?

Like most aristocracy, the antlered animals are sensitive to abuse. They must be killed with due respect, quickly and cleanly. The hunter who hurries and fires a shot that merely wounds sets off an instant, explosive, and emotional glandular reaction in the animal. The body chemistry flashes changes in the fight for life. Adrenaline pours into the blood stream, rushing to every tissue. Enzymes shift to red alert. Secretions of nerve endings in muscle and membrane are altered.

The chemical balance of an animal hunted long and hard is different from the one killed quickly. True, no hunter can make every shot perfect; but there's little excuse for not

23

trying. The animal best killed for the table is the one that never knew what hit it.

The most commonly hunted antlered animals in the United States are the whitetail and mule deer, the elk, the moose, and the pronghorn antelope. The fact that the pronghorn isn't a true antelope makes little difference. All are magnificent trophy animals and rank with the finest food ever to grace a table, when the carcasses are handled properly.

The foresighted hunter of the antlered fellows includes a field dressing pack in his gear. Neatly and compactly put together, the weight of the pack is negligible. It can be stashed within easy distance and moved whenever the hunter lengthens his range.

A few hunters with extremely rare skill may be able to field dress a larger carcass with little more than a large, sharp pocket knife. But most of us require a pack that includes: a sharp hunting knife; thirty to forty feet of light but strong rope; an ample supply of wiping and sacking cloths—it should be porous, such as muslin from old sheeting, without loose fibers that will embed in the meat; black pepper to shoo away the insects; and a small meat saw in case the carcass has to be quartered in the field. A handsaw will bind, and quartering with a hand axe will leave splinters of bone in the meat.

Roll the field dressing tools in a piece of lightweight plastic tarp, making a neat and easily carried package. The sheet of plastic should, when spread, cover an area on the ground a little larger than the carcass of the animal being hunted. The tarp will be worth many times its weight, especially when the ground is muddy or snow-slushy. Spread the plastic, roll the carcass onto it, and a clean working surface is provided on any ground conditions.

The best table meat is field dressed at the moment of kill, but a word of caution to the novice. Don't dash, off guard, upon a big game animal that may be merely wounded or stunned. A few points of desperate, angered antler rearing up in a hunter's face makes for a very unpleasant moment.

24

And don't pull the knife and start whacking away because the job is best done quickly. The contents of a perforated stomach will taint the meat. Field dressing offers few opportunities to undo mistakes. Proceed rapidly—with discipline and care.

Bleeding

Bleeding the kill is the first order of business.

There are hunters, including those with long experience, who hold that the wound from a high-powered bullet plus blood loss during field dressing are sufficient for proper bleeding. This opinion is not substantiated by the findings of nutritional scientists working in controlled laboratory conditions.

Blood left standing in a cooling carcass tends to seep into tissues, altering the taste in proportion to the amount of blood and acting as a culture for certain types of bacteria. Play it safe and get rid of all blood possible—while the body heat is still at its peak.

The carcass may be hung by its hind legs for bleeding, using a tree limb for support. Tie a rope to each hind leg and haul the carcass off the ground, keeping the legs spread. Or use a gambrel stick. This simple device is made from a section of limb or sapling strong enough to support the carcass. Cut it a couple of feet long, sharpen the ends, and insert the sharpened ends in either hind leg through cuts made between the bone and main tendons just above the hocks. The gambrel, useful in handling several types of game, securely spreads the hind legs and provides a support for hanging.

If the carcass is too large to hang, place its head as steeply downhill as possible for bleeding.

The Handy Gambrel

When the trophy is of no value, bleeding is simple. Sever the throat by inserting the knife at the base of the ear behind the jaw and cut outward.

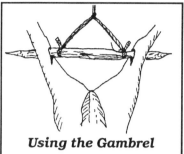

Using the Gambrel

The hunter who wants the trophy must keep the cape intact. He may choose one of several bleeding methods:

Make the cut at the point of the brisket where the neck joins the chest. This cut will sever the blood vessels and permit the knife to enter the heart and lung cavity.

Or insert the knife through the rib cage a few inches behind the joint of the left foreleg, cutting the large blood vessels connecting the heart and lungs.

Professional taxidermists offer a tip for a third method which can be used if circumstances permit removal of the head at this stage. Make the initial skin cut for removal of the cape, as detailed herein in the "trophies" chapter. Peel the cape far enough to expose the midsection of the neck. Then simply cut the head off. Bleeding will occur through the neck stump. The head and portion of severed neck is hung, snout upward, with the loose portion of cape still attached. The trophy portion drains while work continues on the carcass. Salt down the trophy section for short-term preservation. The peeling chore may be com-

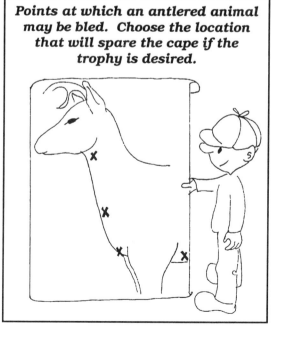

Points at which an antlered animal may be bled. Choose the location that will spare the cape if the trophy is desired.

pleted later either by hunter or taxidermist. If delays in delivery to the taxidermist seem likely, the trophy section should be frozen for safe keeping as soon as possible.

Whatever technique is used, bleeding cuts should be deep, clean, and kept open to insure good drainage.

Gland Removal

Deer have glands on their hind legs that most hunters refer to as "musk" glands. These are the tarsals and metatarsals. The tarsals are located on the inner parts of the hind legs at about the hocks, one gland on each leg. The metatarsals are positioned about halfway down the legs on the outside.

The tarsals play an important part in the sex life of the deer, giving off a musk. In some varieties, bucks and does bend their legs together and curve their bodies so that they urinate on the hair tufts covering the glands. The compounded perfume turns shy does into wantons and revitalizes the virility of decrepit old bucks.

Locate and remove the glands of any animal that may, in handling, taint the meat.

If a hunter never touches these glands with his hands or knife, he can successfully dress out an animal without de-glanding it. The glands cease functioning at death. In themselves they will not affect the taste of the meat. But anything touching the "musk" glands is tainted, and the taint transfers with a secondary touch to the meat. The taint permeates the meat and is almost a guarantee of a gamy steak, roast, or stew.

The glands vary in size and hair-patch characteristics according to the breed. They range from about one to five inches in length. Their distinguishing hair patch may be fringed with white hair, show a difference in grain or growth pattern, or sport a small bald spot at the center.

The hunter with a keen nose has yet another tool for locating the "musk" glands, his sense of smell. Usually a few close-up exploratory sniffs is all that's needed.

Two primary rules govern the de-glanding of all game animals. First, be sure to remove the entire gland, intact, taking the necessary patch of skin and flesh.

Second, hands and knife must be cleansed before touching the carcass again. Otherwise the musk will be transferred to the meat, defeating the very purpose of the de-glanding operation. This can be quite a problem on a cold, blustery day when no water is nearby. A simple solution is to slip a pair of the cheap, disposable plastic gloves into a pants or jacket pocket before going into the field. Use the gloves and a sharp pocket knife for the de-glanding operation. Throw away the gloves and retire the knife from further service until it can be cleaned.

Evisceration (Removal of the Entrails)

Nobody likes this chore. With an icy wind knifing his back and a mass of steaming innards staring him in the face, the hunter may well wonder if it's all worth the comforts of home.

The best medicine for the misery is to get on with the job. Unless unusual circumstances absolutely force a delay, there's no time like the present. Wildlife scientists recommend gutting within the hour after the animal is killed. Microbes in the rumen continue to work, producing an undesirable gaseous condition. Bloating of the viscera makes it much more difficult to dress out a clean carcass suitable for human consumption.

Animals are gutted with a variety of successful techniques, and one hunter's system is as good as another's if the results are first rate. The goal is to remove the viscera (entrails) from gullet to anus all in a piece without puncturing anything.

If the animal has been gut-shot, prompt evisceration must include trimming out contaminated areas of meat and washing of the body cavity with cold water and wiping cloths.

It's important to keep animal hair from direct contact with the meat. Keep the edges of the belly hide rolled back when the body cavity is opened. If preferred, remove a strip of hide a couple of inches wide from crotch to throat, along the line where the cut to open the body cavity will be made.

The conventional method of gutting, approved by the animal science departments of numerous state universities, begins with the animal on its back. (Prop the sides with stones or brush to keep the carcass from wobbling.) The hide is slit from anus to sternum, the breast bone. Don't cut beneath the hide. Roll the edges back to keep the carcass clean and expose the wall of abdominal muscles.

Cut around the pizzle and between the testicles if the kill is male. Detach the pizzle, leaving enough for sex identification.

Next, circle the rectum with a shallow cut about half an inch outside the perimeter of the rectum. Deepen this cut carefully, staying against the bone that surrounds the pelvic area. The anus, or rectum, is the outer ending of the colon, and the purpose of this cut is simply to free the colon, missing the bladder. When the colon and anus are freed, pull a length of colon outside the animal and tie it off to keep feces from contaminating the carcass.

Open the body cavity by first making a small slit in front of the pelvis. Slip the fingers of the free hand into the opening, using them to closely follow the knife, pressing down and protecting the innards as the cut progresses straight up the belly to the sternum. This cut is made with the sharp edge of the knife blade upward, the tip slicing through the abdominal muscle wall.

The rib cage is separated with a deeper cut just off center of the breast bone. A sharp knife will cut the cartilage

29

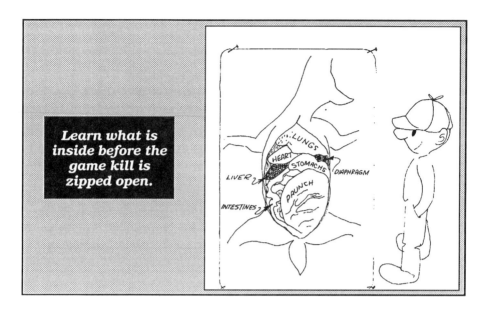

Learn what is inside before the game kill is zipped open.

binding the ribs to the sternum; or the breast bone may be parted with a saw.

The non-trophy kill is cut on up the neck to the chin. When the trophy is valued, the body-opening cut stops just forward of the brisket to keep from ruining the cape.

With the body laid open from butt to bumper, return to the butt area, reach inside the carcass, and gently pull the anus and previously tied-off colon through the pelvis. If the anus was properly cut from the outside, it will pull into the opened body cavity quite easily.

Start opening the body cavity in the pelvic area.

Pull and roll the intestines out, working toward the breast bone. Little cutting is necessary. A large blood vessel attaches the liver to the back and a small cut will free it. Keep the liver cool and clean for tasty eating.

The liver is a good clue to the physical condition of the animal. It should be uniform in color and free from lesions. If its appearance raises questions, show it to a wildlife officer.

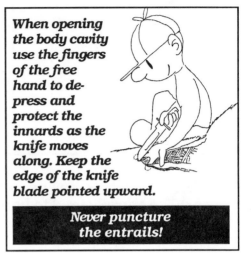

When opening the body cavity use the fingers of the free hand to depress and protect the innards as the knife moves along. Keep the edge of the knife blade pointed upward.

Never puncture the entrails!

With the liver removed, the entrails remain attached by the gullet (esophagus). Cut the gullet loose, clamping with the fingers and tying off to keep the stomach contents from leaking and imparting a wild taste to the meat. If the cape is still intact, the hunter has no choice but to work up inside the neck in freeing gullet and windpipe.

Cut around the diaphragm to free heart and lungs. Save the heart if desired.

An alternative gutting method starts with the carcass being turned a hundred and eighty degrees from its bleeding position. The forequarters are positioned uphill, shifting the weight of the viscera toward the rear. The carcass is positioned on its back. The body cavity is opened from crotch to neck—to brisket if the trophy is being saved—exercising the degree of care already emphasized. The gullet and windpipe are freed first. The gullet is tied off and the entrails are loosened and spilled from the body cavity, working from front to rear. The colon is freed at the pelvis and tied off, completing the operation.

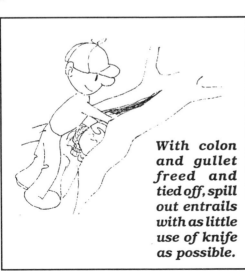

With colon and gullet freed and tied off, spill out entrails with as little use of knife as possible.

31

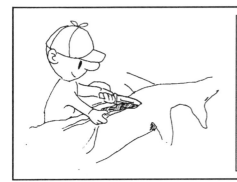

Continue the body-opening cut all the way to the throat, or to the brisket if the cape must be left intact for trophy purposes. Veer slightly off center at the breast bone to sever cartilage.

The nasty job is not as complicated as it might first appear. The entrails tend to hang together and slither out of the body cavity. Concentration and diligence are tools secondary only to the knife.

The eviscerated cavity must be wiped clean of blood. Separate the pelvic bones for wider spreading of the hind legs for faster cooling. Speed up cooling also by propping the body cavity open with sticks.

The colon may be freed from outside. Cut around the rectum carefully, working the blade inward against the pelvic bones to avoid puncturing the colon. When freed, a length of colon may be easily pulled out and tied off.

If the carcass cannot be immediately hung or skinned, drag it onto a cushion of brush, permitting better air circulation to carcass. Everything possible must be done to speed up loss of body heat.

Don't spill the contents when freeing the gullet!

Skinning

Certain circumstances may rule out immediate removal of an animal's head, legs, and hide. Perhaps the situation forces the hunter to drag the carcass. He must loosely pack the gutted body cavity with clean wiping cloths, slit the hide in several places close to the edges of the crotch-to-throat body opening, and temporally re-close the cavity with a rough lacing of cord or cloth strips. This protects the body cavity from foreign matter while the carcass is being dragged. The hair growth points toward the rear; so drag the carcass head first, if it

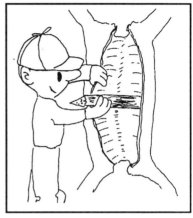

must be dragged at all—and remember that every bump, rock and snag is bruising the finest meat in the world. Don't forget to cover the antlers or flag them with a red bandanna to caution other hunters.

Early skinning has two strong advantages. It speeds up the cooling process. The skin comes off much more easily when the body heat is high.

The idea that the skin should be left on to keep the meat from drying out is mostly an old bogey, an example of the chaff that seeps into the lore of any wood and field sport.

Nutritional experts with specialized knowledge of the subject punch several holes in the old argument.

1. Negligible moisture loss is less important than possible taste alteration due to retardation of the cooling process.

2. Game meat tends to glaze with a moisture retaining coating immediately after it's skinned.

3. In any event, the meat is going to hang skinless for several days of aging.

Since large animals, such as elk and moose, lose heat slowly because of sheer size, wildlife experts in big-game states mince no words about the importance of early skinning.

"The main secret in getting good elk meat is to skin and quarter the animal as soon as possible for the quicker elk meat cools out, the better it will taste," says a wildlife information chief. "It is almost impossible to cool out an elk quickly enough without skinning it. Quartering it will add to the speed of cooling and is also important for transporting. A man can carry one quarter on his back and a pack animal can carry two quarters, one on each side of the pack saddle."

This expert view on skinning is of course applicable to all wild game.

Large or small, the animal skin is cut down the inside length of each leg. These cuts join the crotch-to-neck cut that opened the body cavity for gutting. The leg cuts extend out to the knee joints of the front legs and the hocks of the hind legs. The legs may be cut off at this time, forelegs at knees, hind at hocks. If not, cut around the legs at those points to separate the skin. Circle the neck with a cut that intersects the crotch-to-throat cut. For the trophy animal, make this intersecting cut further back, close to the shoulders and point of the brisket. These cuts combine to leave the animal in a "blanket" of hide that's opened inside the legs, along the underbelly and around the neck, or shoulders in, the case of the trophy animal.

34

The large animal, too bulky to hang, is quartered and skinned or skinned on the ground whole.

To quarter: Halve the animal by cutting straight across the body between the first and second rib, counting from the back. Then separate each half by sawing straight down the backbone.

If convenient, hang the quarters for skinning.

To skin the large carcass whole, turn the animal on one side. Start with the legs. Peel the top side rear and front legs. Then peel the body skin off of the upper side and as far down along the back as possible, pressing the meat down with one hand and pulling the skin toward the back, working back and forth along the length of the carcass. Keep rolling the hide back as it comes loose. When one side of the carcass is skinned, spread the loose skin away from the animal like a protective blanket on to which the carcass can be rolled. Cut off the tail under the hide, leaving it attached, roll the carcass over and repeat the operation on the un-skinned side.

Basic Skinning Cuts:
The long body cut
opened the animal
for evisceration (gut-
ting). After eviscera-
tion add cuts to ring
the legs and neck;
then open the skin
on the inner sides of
legs, joining the pre-
viously made cuts.

A hanging carcass is more conveniently skinned. So when the size of the animal and availability of an overhead support (such as a tree limb) permit, by all means hang the animal. It is preferable to hang it head-down, from a gambrel or with ropes knotted to the legs. If the legs are cut off before hanging, be sure to leave enough below the hocks to secure the gambrel.

With the described skinning cuts made, peel out all four

35

legs. Cut off the tail, leaving it attached. At the rump, pull

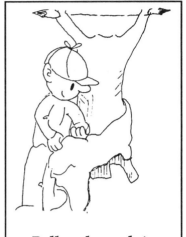

Pull and punch to remove the skin.

the skin far enough from the flesh to permit your other hand inside the pocket between the flesh and skin. Make a hard fist with the "pocket" hand. Use the fist between the hide and meat to drive the hide loose while tugging the hide downward with the other hand. Pulling and punching, work the skin free down to the skin cut encircling the neck or shoulders, as the case maybe. This frees the hide in a single piece.

Use the knife sparingly. This pull-and-fist method will result in a superior hide, free of holes and wads of flesh, both the result of using the knife too freely. If started when the body heat is high, pull-and-fist disrobes an animal quickly.

Protect dressed carcass or quarters with black pepper to discourage insects and a loose covering of porous material.

Never cover with material that will cut off air circulation.

Quarter the carcass with meat saw and knife.

In temperatures below forty degrees the dressed meat may be hung at the campsite for several days. Keep it shaded, never exposed to direct sunlight.

Once body heat dissipates, any temperature above thirty-eight degrees presents a danger to the meat within a few hours, and unduly warm weather, as we noted previously, must be considered when the hunt is in its planning stages. Is it reasonable to expect the most of game meat after abuse by conditions that would have turned a veal chop maggoty?

Complete and early field dressing is always best for the meat. If the situation in the field prohibits the full routine, prompt bleeding, gutting, and cooling of un-skinned game are minimum essentials.

Sack skinned carcass or quarters with porous material for transporting. Skinned or un-skinned, keep the meat cool and clean during its journey home. Aging, butchering, preserving, and cooking will be looked at in later chapters.

4 *Other Big Critturs*

The hunter experienced in field handling one type of American big game can transfer his talents to a differing variety without great difficulty.

4 | *Other Big Critturs*

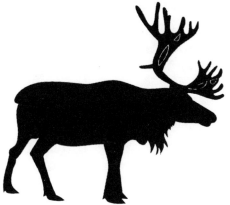

T he family *cervidae*, deer, was chosen as the example for a detailed primer of field dressing because among the large animals it covers the widest range and is the most popularly hunted.

Conveniently for hunters, the Creator sketched the design for most quadrupeds, four-legged animals, in closely related outlines. It follows that they are field dressed with the basic techniques we have seen. Common sense is always involved, even when animals are cousins in the same family, but the differences in size, weight, hair, eye pupil, etc. are superficial.

Consider the bear:

He's bled with a cut of the jugular or other main artery.

He's opened down the middle of the belly side.

The breast and pelvic bones are cut in two.

He's gutted with the colon freed at the anus and tied off.

His gullet is freed and tied off with equal care.

He's skinned with leg cuts joining the long belly cut.

From Bullet to Table

The procedures should sound familiar by now, offering a note of encouragement. The hunter experienced in field handling one type of American big game can transfer his talents to a differing variety without great difficulty.

One big crittur who requires special attention is sus scrofa, commonly known as European wild hog or wild boar. He's an ornery, fearsome fellow, described often as "living in a state of constant rage." He's hunted in several states while his much smaller cousin, the collared peccary, ranges in a relatively very small area in the southwest.

Most tastes find old boar too tough and strong. But a younger wild hog is another platter entirely. Hunting wild hog was a favorite pastime of our European forebears, and his meat on royal tables was a commonplace delight.

Sus scrofa is perhaps the most dangerous game animal found in the United States. He has none of the patience or hesitancy of the bear. He will attack at the slightest provocation, often from a cover of brush, slashing with tusks that may be nine inches long. He is agile, strong, entirely vicious, one animal against which the hunter hasn't all the odds.

Native to Asia and Europe, the wild hog was introduced in the United States by wealthy sportsmen. Fifty of the animals were brought from the Black Forest of Germany in 1893 to stock the private game preserve of Austin Corbin in the Blue Mountains of New Hampshire. In 1900 another importation was released in New York's Adirondack Mountains. An Englishman, George Moore, stocked his private game preserve in the Tennessee Smoky Mountains in 1910. Two years later, a group of wild hogs was imported from Russia to a private preserve at Hooper's Bald in the mountains of Western North Carolina. These were fenced in a six hundred-acre area and no hunting was permitted for eight years. In 1920 many of the hogs escaped through the fence during the wild melee that started out as a European-style hunt with the hunters relying on horses and spears.

Although they like to wallow in mud for relief from heat and insects, wild hogs are generally cleaner than their domesticated relatives. Like their relatives, they will eat just about anything from acorns to snakes, although they prefer to root for tubers. They are extremely intelligent, in cold weather scooping out beds in protected areas and piling up mounds of branches and grasses for warmth.

At any rate, the boar hunter with good aim (it had better be; a full-grown boar can move almost as fast as a deer) must act expediently to save the meat. Although the wild hog is leaner, thinner, and more muscular than the domestic, the fat goes rancid quickly, permeating the meat.

The wild hog hunter must go out prepared to handle an animal that may scale three hundred and fifty pounds on the hoof. (The record kill hit about six hundred pounds.) Bleeding, as usual, is the first tribulation on the docket. For this, the tail end must be as much higher as possible than the tusk end. Hang the carcass head down from a gambrel if possible. Otherwise, position the head down slope and raise the hindquarters, supporting the rump with rocks or chunks of wood.

While wild boars aren't accorded trophy status by the Boone and Crockett Club, the hunter may want a head mounted anyway. If so, bleed the carcass by cutting off the head close to the shoulders, first loosening a plentiful flange of skin behind the line of cut. Pull the skin flange forward until the naked neck is exposed where it joins the body. Then cut through the naked meat. Salt down the head with its skirt of skin and transfer at the first opportunity to a strong brine preservative solution for early delivery to the taxidermist.

If the trophy isn't valued, cut the jugular vein by sticking the knife in the left side of the neck at a point about three inches behind the jaw bone. Work the knife around in the gullet until the rate of blood flow indicates rupture of the big vein.

Gutting closely follows the basic procedures, with a variant detail or two worthy of note.

Begin with a long belly cut from crotch to neck. Exercise

care, cutting no deeper than the guts-casing membrane. The membrane is readily recognizable as layers of belly fat are sliced apart.

Sever the large intestine as close to the anus as possible. Pull the end free and tie it off with a stout cord. Make sure the gullet is free. Then carefully slice the guts-casing membrane, starting at the anus end. The entrails will fall from a hanging carcass with little trouble. Spill them sideways from a prone carcass with a pressure from the hands.

Next, remove internal organs not included with the viscera.

Use extreme care in cutting out the gall bladder.

Edible parts from the interior, if desired, include the heart, liver, kidneys, and small intestine. These parts should have valves, veins, and arteries trimmed off. Rinse them in cold water. Trim away the flap on either side of the long belly cut as well as the fat that held the intestines. Nowadays, this fat is useless. Once, it was rendered into lard, a prized commodity.

The boar refuses to shed his skin as easily as most animals. He can be scalded and scraped, a laborious process not amenable to the welfare of the meat because it delays the loss of body heat. The simplest method is to hang the carcass tail downward. Cut through the skin straight down the back on a line paralleling the spine. Then peel off the skin in strips about as wide as a man's palm, cutting through the skin each time. Pare the carcass to elbows and knees and then cut off the feet, which may be saved for eating. When the carcass cannot be hung, the work should proceed with an old sheet or plastic tarp protecting the meat from direct contact with loose dirt and twigs on the ground.

To halve the carcass in the field, saw it along the center of the spine. This is the best time to remove the tenderloin. It nestles on either side of the backbone cavity. Start at the back end and use one hand to pull it free while the other slices it loose.

Kept cool, clean, protected by porous sacking and black pepper repellant, the kill may be carted home for further operations.

5 *Eatin' Varmints*

The Bedrock Law of Field Handling:

Bleed it.
Gut it.
Cool it.
Keep it cool.
Keep it clean.

5 | *Eatin' Varmints*

Early settlers had the habit of using up everything. Varmints weren't excepted. When a log cabin dweller trapped or shot a pesky little crittur, he usually profited in several ways. He protected the chicken house or carrot crop; he dressed out a pelt for barter or a smidgin of hard cash; and very often he put a tasty dish on the table. Nowadays the hunter may not be worrying about the safety of his chickens and carrots, and the value of most small pelts has deflated. The taste remains, enticing the hungry woodsman and piquing the palate of the gourmet.

Hunters sometimes are a trifle more careless with small carcasses than with the big game kill, perhaps because the little fellow is less impressive. But the small kill requires the same, or even more, detailed attention in field handling. Meat from many of the small varieties tends to spoil very quickly. The bedrock laws of field handling still hold:

Bleed it.
Gut it.
Cool it.
Keep it cool.
Keep it clean.

49

Opossum

The possum is the only pouched animal in North America. It has practically no brains, but has survived seventy million years, since it shared the habitat with the dinosaur.

A favorite small game animal, the possum is hunted almost as avidly as the raccoon. A good coon dog in most instances will tree a possum with all the energetic interest shown the coon.

The possum's ability to feign death in times of danger is his best known trait. "Playing possum" is an idiom deeply rooted in our language. But the animal rarely uses the ploy. The majority flee to safety, dashing down a hole or up a tree. If cornered, they will face their attacker with strings of saliva emitted from their large, wide-opened mouths.

As quickly as possible following the kill, sever the jugular to bleed the possum.

Then remove the musk glands from under the forearms. Take care not to spread the musky contaminant.

Cut the carcass open, from crotch to throat.

Strip out the entrails.

Cut off the head.

Hang the carcass upside down, spreadlegged.

Cut the skin right around the legs close to the feet.

Split the skin down the inside of each leg.

Peel out the legs, then the body.

(In lieu of skinning, the possum can be scalded and scraped. Dip the intact carcass in boiling water, before the viscera is removed, and scrape off the hair from tail to neck with a dulled blade. The procedure is not recommended when fine table meat is the goal.)

Soak the dressed carcass overnight in very cold water to which has been added a baking size Irish potato, grated, and a level tablespoon each of salt and soda.

Remove possum and wipe dry. Dissect the carcass by removing the legs at the main joints and splitting the body straight along the spine. Sprinkle the pieces lightly with finely crushed dry parsley flakes. Wrap each piece individually and pack them overnight in ice, but don't freeze.

The meat is now ready for cooking.

Rabbit

This innocuous fellow must at times feel that everything in the world is stacked against it. Rainstorms kill the young. A field fire destroys the nests. Fresh litters are plowed under and chopped up by farm and lawn machinery. Snowstorms immobilize adults when their need to seek food is desperate. And every meat-eater, including man, devours bunnies by the millions.

Yet the hardy little animal goes on, gaining recognition as a national institution when private club waitresses had their rumps decorated with cute cottontails. Hunters spend more time and money shooting rabbits than for any other species of American game. The rabbit ranges almost everywhere, and despite the hazards faced from birth, it multiplies so rapidly that it is rarely in short supply.

Dashing in and out of cover with blinding speed, the rabbit is a challenge to any shot-gunner. On the table, rabbit meat is such a delight that stocks of domestic rabbit rarely last long in supermarket meat counters.

Because of parasites and parasitic infections, wild rabbits must always be handled with caution. Never feed any internal organs of a rabbit to a hunting dog. Many hunters toss the liver of a freshly killed rabbit to a dog as a reward. Some reward. No better exposure to tapeworm can be imagined.

Rabbits, as if they didn't have trouble in plenty, are also the host of plaguing botflies which lay their eggs deep in the rabbit fur. The hatched larvae burrow into the rabbit's skin and develop into lumps, readily recognizable, called warbles. The warbles emerge and set off to botfly other rabbits. Those who don't are usually killed by cold weather. Warbles are not known to affect the meat, but the hunter should pass up the bunny with the warbly skin.

The most dreaded disease that can be passed from rabbit to man is tularemia, so named because it was first noticed in Tulare County, California. Afflicted rabbits are lethargic and unable to run when disturbed. Any strangely acting rabbit should be shot and buried or burned—and never touched with the bare hands. The parasite has to enter the human blood stream by a break in the skin.

Luckily, tularemia is not common, and today's mycin-type drugs can cure the disease in human beings.

The hunter who uses his head for something more than a support for an ear-flapped cap will stuff a pocket with disposable plastic gloves before taking the field. If the skin on the hands is unbroken, there's little risk in handling rabbit. But why take any risk at all when the alternative is so cheap and simple?

Gut the rabbit as soon as it is killed. This is done by making a single cut down the middle of the belly and spilling out and detaching the entrails.

The rabbit is one of the easiest of all wild animals to skin—unless the hunter tears the fur and the hair starts flying. The naked meat attracts free hair like magnetized glue and the result can be a mess.

To keep the pelt intact, hang bunny spreadlegged, head down. Cut circles around the legs close to the feet and join

Divide the rabbit's skin into pants and jacket. It can then be undressed by pulling the hands in opposite directions.

these to the belly cut with incisions down the middle of the insides of the legs, the cutting pattern we have already so often seen.

Peel out the legs, cut off the tail under the skin to leave it attached, and un-jacket the body by pulling the skin downward. When the pelt is of no value, the simplest way to skin the rabbit is to separate the pelt in two halves with a single cut running right around the body. This cut should be located about halfway between

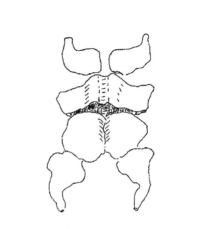

Remove legs and divide bodies of small carcasses.

neck and tail. It should join the belly cut, going from one edge of the belly cut perpendicular across the body and rejoining the belly cut.

Facing the rabbit's back, grasp the edges of the skin-halving cut, one edge in either hand, the knuckles of the hands pointed toward each other. Now by merely holding onto the loosened skin edges and pulling the hands apart, the skin is peeled off. It's as if one hand had shucked the rabbit's pants while the other divested the undershirt and sweater. Disrobe the bunny right down to his feet and head and cut them off.

Section the cleaned carcass by removing the legs at the upper joints and cutting the back into two pieces. Wash in cold, salty water, wipe dry, and pack in ice overnight. The shorter the period between gutting and icing, the better the meat.

Raccoon

The coon is one of the most clever and most adaptable of small animals, and at times in coon history the traits were taxed to their utmost in the struggle for survival.

Capable of making a variety of sounds, coons apparently enjoy conversing with each other. Perhaps their folklore includes the tale of those strange two-legged creatures with the crazy compulsion to wear coonskin coats during the jazz-age. The era witnessed the decimation of the raccoon population, with the price of pelts peaking at about eighteen dollars each.

Conservationists lobbied for protective laws and moved healthy adults to repopulate areas where coons had disappeared. The coon hunter today reaps the benefits. There is hardly an area of the United States where coon may not be found.

The coon offers both food and pelt. Wild-game gourmets relish a coon-graced table, and the coonskin cap has never quite lost its popularity.

Bleeding is of singular importance. The jugular must be opened and the animal hung by its hind feet for thorough bleeding during the earliest possible instant after the kill. Otherwise, the meat spoils rapidly or becomes too gamy for enjoyable eating.

If the pelt is valued, the coon should be skinned before gutting, even as it is bleeding.

Cutting just through the skin, circle the fore feet at the first joints. Join these cuts with a cut running down the insides of the legs and across the chest. Circle the hind feet at their first joints and join these cuts with a skin-deep incision

Make a vise from a couple of sticks to solve the problem of slipping the raccoon's tail from the bone in order to keep the pelt intact for a coonskin cap. With the sticks positioned and the coon's feet secured, a steady pressure will slide the tailskin free.

running down the inner sides of the hind legs and across the pelvic region. Open the skin on the belly side of the carcass all the way from the anus to throat. Cut around the tail on the **bottom side only**, joining this short, semicircular cut to the cut connecting the extremities of the hind legs and peel the legs. Loosen the edges of the belly cut and the cut underneath the tail.

Now the carcass is turned around, its back facing the hunter, its head still hanging downward. Work the skin loose around the stump of the tail. Then take two strong but thin sticks about eight or ten inches long and place a stick on either side of the exposed tailbone stump. Position the sticks at right angles to the tail, with the tailbone between the sticks about midway in their lengths. By gripping the ends of the sticks in either hand and clamping each pair of ends together, the hunter forms a "vise" at the root of the tailbone. A firm and even pressure will now slip the tailskin intact off the bone. Be careful not to pull the tail off or tear the pelt.

The body skin is now removed, using a sharp knife only where necessary, with the skin carefully worked off of the head, trimming off the ears on the underside of the pelt and easing the skin carefully from around eyes and lips.

And hold everything right there for a moment.

The musk glands must now be removed. They are pear-shaped, one under each forearm. Without their careful and unbroken removal the animal will not be fit to eat.

Next, split the carcass open from crotch to throat, being careful not to puncture the intestines. Remove viscera and inner organs. Cut off the head, naked tailbone, and feet. Split the carcass in half cutting the length of the spine.

The carcass may now be soaked overnight in cold water which contains a small amount of salt and soda. This draws out vestigal blood. Or an alternate method may be preferred: salt the carcass all over lightly. Then place the salted meat on a sieve or any kind of grille that will permit water to drip out. Leave the carcass overnight in a cool, dry place. Wash the treated carcass thoroughly in cold water and pack it in ice for at least one day before cooking.

Squirrel

In these days when the American conscience is nitpicking its past, why not credit the squirrel with its contribution to American victory in the Revolutionary War? It might have been indirect. An army of squirrels surely didn't rout the British. But the squirrel was a very real contribution, nevertheless.

In nearly every case better equipped than the raggle-taggle colonist, the British infantryman was a sacrificial offering to the American shooting eye when small arms fire crackled. "I can knock a squirrel's eye out at forty feet," was the old frontier boast, and in nearly all cases the speaker meant it literally. From boyhood, he'd developed his marksmanship shooting squirrels. The animals were so plentiful they had to be killed off as pests. They were also good to eat.

A threepence bounty was placed on squirrels in Pennsylvania in 1749 in an effort to control pest damage to crops on wilderness farms. The law had to be repealed the following year, after more than 8,000 pounds of sterling had been collected by squirrel shooters, almost bankrupting the colony's treasury.

The unlucky Redcoat was a child's play target to the squirrel's eye shooter lurking behind a tree stump. So give the squirrel his due as the first, and one of the finest,

Old-timers shucked their squirrels by peeling out the hind quarters and then firmly standing on the tail (which is still attached to pelt), grasping the rear legs and exerting a strong steady pull on the legs with the hands. The squirrel will shed its coat wrong side out.

56

American army training devices.

The squirrel kill may be handled equally well in several ways. Gut it first with the usual crotch to throat cut. Sever jugular to bleed. Then circle legs with cuts above the feet. Open the skin with the standby cut up and down the legs. Peel out the legs and then strip off the pelt, which is stuck pretty tight.

Or, bleed and gut. Then open the skin around the body in a line perpendicular to the spine. Loosen the edges of the two sections of body skin, grasp with the hands and shuck off the skin by pulling the hands away from each other, as with the rabbit.

Or, remove the skin first with a simple procedure preferred by many hunters. Simply peel out the hind legs, open the skin across the rump, and cut the tail loose underneath the skin, leaving the tail attached securely to the pelt. Now lay the carcass on firm ground, belly side up, plant a foot on the tail, grasp the hind legs, and pull with a steady pressure on the legs. The skin will come off to the head and front legs like a kid whipping off a pullover sweater. Peel out the front legs. Cut off the head, or peel it out, depending on whether or not a trophy mounting is desired.

The squirrel is much more reluctant to surrender its skin than the rabbit so be prepared for the extra effort. Quick loss of body heat and the blood are important. As soon as bleeding is through and most of the body heat dissipated, soak the carcass for several hours in moderately salted water at a temperature below forty degrees, with a tablespoon of dry sage stirred into the water just before the soaking process begins.

Woodchuck

Legend has it that the woodchuck (groundhog) is the weather forecaster of the animal kingdom. If it comes out of its burrow on Groundhog Day and sees its shadow, it snuggles back to hibernate another six weeks; if it doesn't, spring is just around the corner. The last known chuck to follow its own prediction stayed out—and almost froze to death in the worst blizzard of winter.

Even though its extra sensory powers are mythical, the chuck's reputation as a tasty dish isn't.

Bleed the carcass quickly, severing the jugular or cutting off the head. Now examine the anus where three glands may be readily seen protruding after the animal has been killed. Excise these glands instantly, taking care to remove them intact. Gut with the crotch-to-neck belly cut. Remove the skin with the usual procedure, ringing the legs with cuts above the feet, opening the skin from feet cuts to belly cut with a cut running down the inside of each leg, peeling out legs, then pelt, cutting off tail under the skin and leaving it attached.

As always, don't forget to trim out bullet damages.

Remove the head and feet.

Cut off the legs at body joints and divide the body in half.

Wash the pieces and soak them for at least twelve hours in very cold water to which has been added one tablespoon of salt per quart of water and, if available, a quarter of a teacup of crushed spicewood twigs.

The chuck is now ready for the cook.

6 The Airborne Creatures

Know your game laws, which may re-quire the retention of an identifying part of a feathered kill.

6 | *The Airborne Creatures*

Again know your game laws, which may require the retention of an identifying part of a feathered kill. And ever again, bear in mind the basic laws of game-handling: Bleed it. Clean it. Cool it. Keep it cool and clean.

Hunters often desire only the breasts of small birds, cutting out the portion and disposing of the rest. To retain whole carcasses of feathered kills, large or small, here are some tips:

For best table meat—and the easiest job of cleaning—a bird should be field dressed while body heat is highest, on the spot if possible. Bleed by cutting the throat or severing the head. Eviscerate by opening the body cavity from breast to anus and stripping out the entrails, using the knife sparingly.

Most birds can be dry plucked while body heat is high. Later, a wet-plucking method may have to be employed, dipping the carcass in very hot water to loosen the feathers. The plucked bird may be "singed" to remove remaining hair-like pin feathers. If skinning is preferred to plucking, take care not to start tearing the meat. This can be avoided if the hunter will note the delicate, transparent membrane between the skin and the meat and use one hand to keep this membrane as intact as possible against the meat while the other hand works in unison to peel the skin off.

De-glanding is a problem of no moment in birds. However, remove the oil sack at the base of the tail; in waterfowl trim out inner fat to reduce the risk of a "fishy" taste.

Wipe the dressed bird with a clean cloth. Wrap in a piece of porous material. The dressed carcass is just as easy to carry as the non-dressed. It should be refrigerated as soon as possible, a need easily filled with a lightweight cooler in car, station wagon, or at the campsite.

Sometimes with a fine pointer working, the pace of the hunt delays full dressing on the spot. The birds should at least be drawn and never stacked, hung, or carried so that air circulation is impeded.

Knowing the approximate age of a bird will help the cook, old and tougher birds requiring a longer cooking time. Excepting waterfowl, if a game bird can be lifted by the lower beak without the beak breaking, the bird is something of a senior citizen and inclined to toughness. In any young bird, the outer end of the breastbone is rather flexible.

Game birds should have at least forty-eight hours aging at a temperature just above freezing to dissipate "gaminess."

7 Butchering

Butchering is an integral part of the hunting ritual.

7 | *Butchering*

Few hunters would holler uncle and back off from a rabbit carcass. But many, experienced as well as novice, hesitate at the prospect of butchering a large carcass and bug out by hiring a professional meat cutter. There are valid reasons: the hunter may not have the time; the hunter may be an apartment dweller with humorless neighbors eying the bloody activity occurring on the terrace or courtyard; and the professional butcher may (or may not) do a better job of cutting the meat.

If self-doubt is the hang-up, forget it. Remember that millions of beef and hog carcasses are readied for supermarket meat counters every day. Thousands of meat cutters are involved, and surely a few are no more mentally and physically competent than the hunter.

Butchering is an integral part of the hunting ritual, and while reading matter alone is no substitute for experience, it's always best to get staffed with a good briefing. Don't be afraid of making a few mistakes at the outset. They probably won't be serious. The "feel" of meat quickly develops and the basic techniques are similar, transferrable from one animal to another.

From Bullet to Table

A professional butcher may be hired to come over and stand by after work, acting as coach until the hunter gets the hang of things. The idea is fine, if the hunter sticks to the letter of the deal. Don't yield to the natural impulse to let the butcher gradually take over, explaining what he is doing as he goes along. Hang in there with the knives and let the butcher explain while **you** go along. That feeling for the meat develops in the hands doing the cutting.

Butchering offers the opportunity for detailed cleaning of any clots of blood, hair, or bullet-damaged meat that might have been previously missed. A vinegar-soaked cloth picks up those very small bits of hair and blood nicely. Proper equipment makes any job easier, and while a few old hands can do a remarkable job with makeshift, it's best to have a minimum consisting of:

An adequate working surface, good solid table or workbench. (The tailgate of a station wagon or pickup truck parked in the shade does nicely, also.)

A couple of sturdy cutting boards.

Steak, chop, and boning knives, very sharp.

Steel or stone to keep them sharp.

A meat saw.

Cleaver—and use it sparingly to keep bone splinters from embedding in the meat.

Keep in mind that firmly chilled, but not frozen, meat cuts best. Also, meat is the most tender when cooking portions are removed with cuts that go across the grain of the meat.

Most larger quadrupeds yield similar cuts of meat and hence are butchered with similar procedures, although the giants, elk and moose, require variations because of their sheer size.

If the deer, pronghorn, or big horn sheep has been transported whole, the carcass is first halved by sawing straight along the center of the spine. This operation is easiest if the carcass is hung with forequarters downward.

Separate the forequarters from each half by cutting between the first and second ribs, leaving one rib on each hindquarter for shape and support. (See illustration)

From the front quarters remove the shanks at the first leg joints below the body. Now further divide the forequarters in a line running front to rear approximately halfway between the spine and bottom of brisket. Cut off lower portions of the ribs just behind the brisket. Then cut off the upper parts of the ribs behind the shoulders.

Now for the hindquarters: Saw off the lower portions of the legs, the hindleg shanks. Remove the rear legs, and then cut the rump portions from the top of each leg.

Next, cut off the flank.

The carcass is now down to a size permitting division into cooking portions, roasts, chops, steaks, ground meat.

Trim out shanks for hamburger.

Reduce brisket to stewing meat.

Cut roasts or steaks from front shoulders.

From portions of ribs taken from forequarters, cut roasts, and stewing meat.

From hind shanks and legs, cut roasts, stew meat, and steaks.

Cut roasts from the rump portions.

From the loin, take sirloin and chops.

Grind the flank for hamburger or reduce it to stewing meat.

The biggies, elk and moose, are halved in the familiar way, by dividing the spine straight along its center. The front and hind quarters are sectioned out with a dividing cut just behind the ribs.

The flank is sliced off as with the smaller animals. With the front quarter laid out before him, the hunter can decide the line through which he will cut off the bottom part of the ribs. The upper rib portion yields rib steaks or rib roasts. The plate (lower portion of ribs) is usually divided into barbecuing ribs or boned out for stew or burger.

On moose and elk, the customary first cut on the hindquarter removes the sirloin tip. First, make a cut on the lower forepart of the hind legs to reveal the knee joints. Detach the kneecaps and cut the meat away from the thigh bone. When the upper joint of the thighbone is reached, cut perpendicular to the thighbone, removing the sirloin tip. The tip is excellent for steaks and roasts. Separate the legs from the loins. The legs yield round steaks and roasts. From the loins cut steaks or roasts. The steaks should look like T-bones, sirloins, porterhouses, and, when the forward end of the loin is reached, club steaks.

In butchering a bear, the simplest procedure is best: halve the carcass, locate the upper leg joints, and remove the hams and shoulders. Trim off the flanks and get rid of excess fatty tissues. Then divide remainder of the carcass into roasts and stewing meat.

The boar requires a few variations which don't greatly complicate butchering. Halve the carcass, with the standard cut along the centerline of the spine. Take out the spareribs by running the knife between the ribs and sidemeat and cutting the cartilage when the base of the ribs is reached. The ribs can be taken out in a section. And they're fine for barbecuing.

Do not divide the wild hog halves into quarters, as with other quadrupeds.

Instead, cut the hocks from the lower parts of the legs. Locate the joints and remove the hams and shoulders. With the remainder of each side: divide the bacon from the loin, determining by examination about where the loin becomes bacon and marking the line with the knife.

The section of the back above the front shoulder is the shoulder butt. Divide the butts from the loins. The forward part of the shoulder butt can also be removed. Butchers call this the jowl butt.

Cutting up birds and small animal carcasses requires little more than a sharp knife and a bit of practice. If the game is to be cooked whole, cut off the head and feet—plus the oil sack at the base of the tail on a bird—clean off any bits of foreign matter and blood clots with cold water, make sure bullet or other damage is trimmed out, and the meat is ready to be cooked whole.

To dissect small animals, remove the legs at the joints and divide the carcass into conveniently small pieces by halving it with a cut straight across the middle. It may then be quartered by dividing each half with cuts straight along each section of spine. A bird carcass is usually reduced by first taking off the legs and wings at the joints. The body is then halved into back and breast sections, with the back and breast further divided as desired.

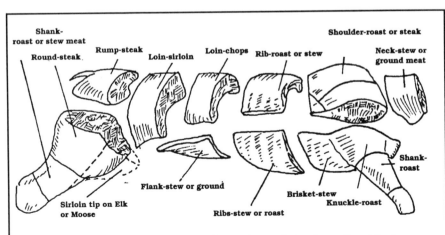

Basic Butchering of Antlered Animals. Note Sirloin Tip removal on the big fellows.

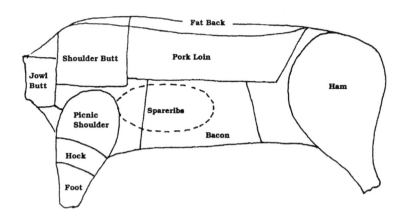

Breaking down the side of wild hog

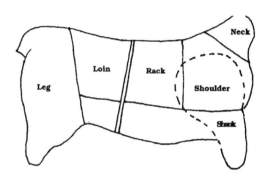

Divide Bighorn

8 Aging and Preserving

Aging cannot undo slipshod field handling but may only compound errors carelessly made immediately after the kill. When the animal dies the meat starts to age, for better or worse.

8 *Aging and Preserving*

Aging dissipates unwanted nuances of taste associated with any animal, game or domestic, and permits enzymes to tenderize the meat by their natural action in the tissue. Proper aging also firms the "set" of the meat, giving it a better cutting quality.

Aging must take place above freezing but at a temperature no higher than thirty-eight degrees. Meat cannot be frozen with the intention of aging it later.

Most small animals, and birds if desired, are best aged for a day or so in salty solution to draw out remaining blood.

Hang the larger carcasses, or their sides or quarters, in a dry, cool place. A walk-in cooler is best because the temperature must be constant. But a tight back porch, garage, or outbuilding will do. Meat quickly picks up odors, and excess moisture increases the development of mold.

The usual practice is to age antlered carcasses for ten days.

However, studies at the University of Wyoming make it questionable whether or not pronghorn antelope should be aged more than a couple of days, if at all, after chilling. The studies involved use of Warner-Bratzler Shear values, which measures tenderness, and revealed that the extremely low shear values of antelope meat aged fourteen days were associated with meat which lacked consistency. Elimination of aging beyond rapid, thorough chilling also helped to prevent bacterial growth.

Wild hog is not "aged" in the usual sense. It should be refrigerated as soon as possible after kill and butchering. Portions not to be cooked and eaten as fresh boar are preserved by methods we'll be looking at shortly.

Aging cannot undo slipshod field handling but may only compound errors carelessly made immediately after the kill. When the animal dies the meat starts to age, for better or worse.

Preserving game meat involves two methods.
1. Freezing
2. Curing

Meat to be frozen should be packaged in meal-sized portions, the amount that will be used at a single cooking. If more than one piece of meat is included in a package, separate each piece with a double thickness of heavy wax paper.

The efficiency of freezing depends in part on how the meat

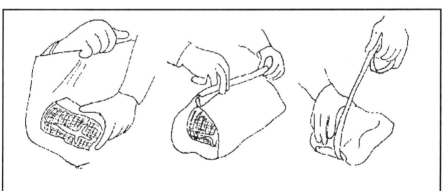

The drugstore wrap for freezing meat. Remove all air possible and seal the portion tightly.

is wrapped and how quickly it's frozen.

Choose the best grade of freezer wrapping and heavy plastic bags for packaging. Hunters sometimes argue the relative meats of the "butcher" wrap as opposed to the "drugstore" wrap. Actually, the way the wrapper is folded is less important than the amount of air left inside the finished package. Fold the wrapper so that all air is excluded and seal the edges airtight. Label and date each package before it goes into the freezer.

Meat should be frozen rapidly at ten degrees below zero. If a home freezer is to be used, turn the control to the coldest setting. Scatter the packages, separating them as much as possible to expose all sides of each package evenly to the freezing temperature. Keep the frozen meat at a zero temperature, or lower. Carefully trim excess fat before freezing in order to retard tendencies to rancidness.

Frozen game meat in the form of steaks, roasts, chops, stewing meat, etc. keeps well for eight to twelve months. Ground meat should not be kept frozen longer than about ten weeks.

Meat should never be permitted to thaw and then re-frozen. Wood smoke and salt are the two basic ingredients commonly used to cure meat. An excellent mixture for brine curing consists of eight pounds of non-iodized salt, two pounds of brown or white sugar, two ounces of saltpeter mixed in four and one-half gallons of pure water.

To purify the water, boil it for five minutes and strain it into another container to remove any sediment. Re-heat the water and stir in the other ingredients until dissolved. Skim the surface and cool the mixture to forty degrees temperature.

Cut the meat into uniform pieces and chill it to a temperature between thirty-four and forty degrees. Pack the meat into a clean crock or wooden barrel. Pour in the brining solution until the meat is well covered. Do not seal the brining container. Cover the top with a piece of cheese cloth.

The meat and brine solution must be kept at a temperature between thirty-four and forty degrees throughout the curing process. Higher temperatures will spoil the meat; lower will retard curing. Curing time for thicker, larger pieces is about three and one half days per pound.

"Jerky" is easily made. Cut the meat to be jerked into strips about an inch wide and half-inch thick, six to twelve inches long. Brine the strips for two days in a solution consisting of one pound of non-iodized salt to each three quarts of pure water. When the meat is removed from the brine, wipe it dry and hang it in bright, direct sunlight to dry. It can be threaded on a string or wire, with the pieces separated in order to expose each piece to maximum air circulation and sunlight. While drying, the meat must be protected from insects with a loose covering of cheesecloth. When completely dehydrated, jerky can be stored for long periods without refrigeration, in a cool, dry place protected from dust and insects.

The simplest method of curing wild hog bacon or ham (or domestic pork for that matter), is to cover the meat with dry, non-iodized salt until it is totally white and let it stand until it takes the salt. Cure the meat on shelving which will permit air circulation. Crude shelving is satisfactory. Make it by laying some slats between stacked bricks. Conditions in the cooling area should imitate the old-time cellar or smokehouse as nearly as possible, cool and dry. Cool, shadowy areas in the garage or workshop will do, or a corner in an unheated section of the basement. If the floor is dirt, so much the better.

About twenty days is required for thorough salt penetration in bacon. A ham needs about one week per inch of thickness.

A dry-cure mixture for that old-time "country" flavor consists of eight pounds of salt, three pounds of brown sugar, three ounces of saltpeter, one ounce each of red and black pepper, and a tablespoon of borax. Rub a third of the mixture into the meat the first day, a third the second, and the remainder the third day. The curing time is the same as for the plain salt treatment.

Any variety of cured game meat may be smoked for better keeping and flavor. Wash the cured meat and let it drip at least twelve hours before smoking it.

A "smokehouse" is easily and cheaply devised.

The smoker is nothing more nor less than an enclosure to keep the smoke in and on the meat. Use any old refrigerator, large barrel or packing case, or a shed that's fairly "smoke tight." Or knock a "box" together out of scrap lumber, similar to the one shown in the illustration. The dimensions are approximate, and finished carpentry is by no means a requirement.

You also will need an ordinary, one-burner electric hotplate, an old skillet or pan, a couple pieces of thin metal such as chimney flashing, a thermometer ten or twelve inches long, a couple of old wire racks similar to those in a stove oven, and a few bricks.

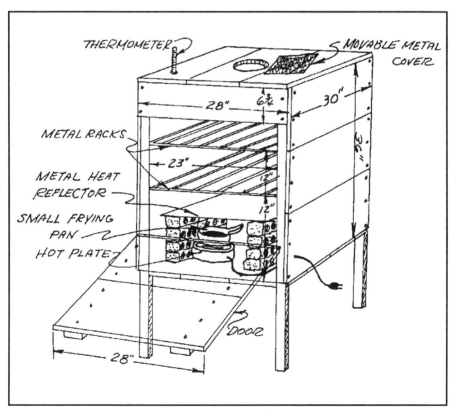

Cut a hole, about three inches in diameter, in the center, of the top of the smoker. Cover the hole with a flat piece of metal. By moving the metal to expose more or less of the hole during the smoking process, the rate of smoke can be controlled.

Make another hole in the top several inches away from the "smoke-draft" hole. This second hole should be just large enough to accommodate the diameter of the thermometer, fitting tightly when the tip of the thermometer is thrust through the hole. Push the tip of the thermometer through the hole into the smoker, leaving only the gauge markings from ninety degrees and upward visible from outside the smoker. Use a bit of putty or tape to seal around the thermometer hole. A glance at the gauged section of thermometer outside the hole will reveal the inside temperature.

Place the hotplate inside the smoker on the center of the base. Place the skillet or pan—a cakepan is fine—on the hotplate. Stack a row of bricks along two sides of the hotplate and pan, allowing several inches between each row and the hotplate. The top of each row should be about five or six inches higher than the level of the pan when it's set on the hotplate. Lay a square piece of thin metal on the brick stacks, forming a heat reflector over the hotplate. If a piece of metal isn't handy, use some stiff wires such as coathanger wire as a "bridge" between the brick stacks to support a heat reflector fashioned from a double thickness of ordinary aluminum foil.

Meat may be hung inside the smoker for curing. Or it may be placed on racks. Mount the racks inside the smoker so that the lowest is about ten inches above the heat reflector.

The smoker is now ready for business. Use nonresinous wood, peeled alder, willow, apple, or hickory to produce the smoke. Reduce the wood to very fine shavings or sawdust. If preferred, hickory dust may be purchased at a commercial curing house or locker plant.

Sprinkle the wood in the pan, turn on the hotplate, and smoke will start to generate shortly. Smoke movement and interior temperature are controlled by advancing or retarding heat from the hotplate and adjusting the opening of the smoke-hole in the top of the smoker.

For cold smoking don't let the interior temperature rise above one hundred degrees. This type of smoking is used for curing. For smoke cooking, keep the temperature at about a hundred and fifty degrees.

Cold smoking to cure meats requires about three days. Meats should be smoked to an amber color. Smoke cooking of large chunks of meat or fish is not recommended, as it is difficult to obtain even and thorough results. Fish larger than a couple of pounds should be filleted. Smaller fish should be split open and laid flat on the racks. Smoke cooking of a one pound fillet requires about seven hours. The smoker is so simple in principle and construction that a little experimentation will quickly acquaint the user with its operation.

9 Trophies

If a dozen or more taxidermists are interviewed, the suggestion is that too many hunters mishandle a trophy in the field because of lack of information or plain carelessness.

9 | *Trophies*

Viewing the trophy as professional artists, taxidermists echo a similar refrain. It adds up to criticisms of much of the material brought to them.

"We can only do the most with what we start with," one long experienced taxidermist puts it, "but a lot of hunters seem to expect more."

If a dozen or more taxidermists are interviewed, the suggestion is that too many hunters mishandle a trophy in the field because of lack of information or plain carelessness.

"They need to get a little more anxious about the tiresome details," the taxidermist says. "For one thing, you can't take a chance with warm weather and not expect the hair to slip. A lot of heads are brought to me that have been frozen for keeping. Freezing's fine as a method of preservation until the trophy can be taken to the taxidermist. But too many have been frozen too late. Soon as the head thaws out, you know it's been carelessly exposed to warm weather and insects. Fellow the other day brought me a deer head, and when it thawed, the antlers pulled fight out of the skull.

"Another thing, we can do some pretty good invisible patching, but we can't do a first class job with a cape that was lacerated when the animal was bled. And on the subject, hunters are sometimes guilty of taking too little cape. Better too much than too little.

"If a hunter wants to peel out the head, fine. But remember that every little tear around the eyes and lips necessitates another invisible repair. The skin must be carefully handled.

"Also, take measurements while the head is intact.

"Finally, the hunter should think of his pocketbook. The single biggest cost factor in preparing a trophy is the taxidermist's working time. The more a hunter contributes to a smooth operation, the less it's likely to cost him."

Without a fairly detailed knowledge of taxidermy, the hunter should hardly plan to have his small animal trophy and eat it too. The difficulty lies in skinning the small animal for both trophy and table fare while retaining certain small bones the taxidermist uses. The coonskin cap is one trophy exception. The hunter may safely skin the coon for table fare and at the same time retain a pelt suitable for tanning and fashioning into headgear.

The bird or small animal may be frozen intact until delivery to the taxidermist.

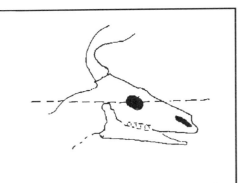

Always leave plenty of material for the taxidermist to work with.

If only the antlers are to be mounted, saw off the section of skull holding the antlers and clean thoroughly by peeling off the skin and washing out the brain matter. Don't cut skimpily. Take off the skull in a single piece from about the top of the eye sockets to the skull's base.

For a full antlered head mounting, the portion of body skin called the cape

84

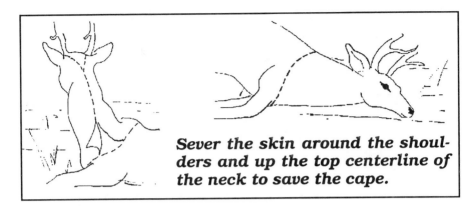

Sever the skin around the shoulders and up the top centerline of the neck to save the cape.

must be sectioned out. Split the skin all the way around the carcass through points between the shoulder blades and the front of the brisket, curving the cut slightly forward to fit the shoulders. Next, starting at the top of the body cut, open the skin straight up the top of the neck with a single cut, stopping at a point six to eight inches below the antlers. From this stopping point, angle cuts to the base of each antler. The trophy can now be peeled off, start at the cut around the forequarters.

When the neck is exposed, it may be severed, the head and attached cape being frozen for later delivery to the taxidermist.

If the hunter desires to complete the skinning of the head, he should first make a few measurements that will be of value to the taxidermist. While the head is intact measure: the distance from the tip of the nose to the front of the eye socket; the distance from the tip of the nose to the back of the ear with the ear in "perked-up" position; the circumference around the neck just below the jawbone.

The taxidermist will use the measurements when making or ordering the head form.

When these measures are noted, proceed to skin out the head by carefully loosening the skin around the antlers and working forward. Cut the ears loose beneath the skin, leaving them attached and take special care in loosening the skin around the eyes, as well as trimming out the lips and nose button. The ears can be peeled out by turning them wrong side out. After the skin has been removed, saw off the antler-retaining section of the skull, taking enough bone to give the antlers a solid base.

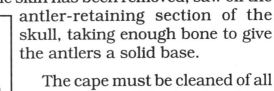

The cape must be cleaned of all bits of flesh and blood. Salt it down thoroughly, raw side up, starting at the middle and rubbing in the salt. Roll the cape, loosely, with the hair side outward for transporting. Never fold a cape with a sharp crease.

For the non-mounted trophy such as a bearskin rug, a couple of variations in the normal skinning procedure are necessary. Make the normal skin cuts down the insides of the legs, joining these with the belly cut from crotch to throat. Work the skin loose around the ankles. When the knife can be inserted between flesh and skin, cut the paws off at the ankle joints, leaving the paws attached, the leg

Peel out the trophy carefully, especially around antlers, eyes, and lips. Sever the ears underneath to leave them attached.

skin unimpaired except for the initial opening cuts down the insides of the legs. Peel off the body skin in one piece until the neck is exposed. Then cut off the head without touching the skin. Remove fatty tissues, clots of blood, and bits of

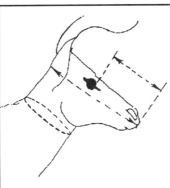

The hunter who intends to peel out the trophy should first take a few simple measurements for the taxidermist's use.

flesh from the inner side of the skin. The paws, head, and body skin will be in a piece, and may be frozen until delivery to the taxidermist.

To remove entire pelt with paws and head (as for a bearskin rug) make the standard skinning cuts, with one variation: Circle only the undersides of the paws and neck. The paws and head may now be removed and left attached to the body pelt. The taxidermist may then peel out paws and head; the result is a complete pelt undamaged from nose to tail.

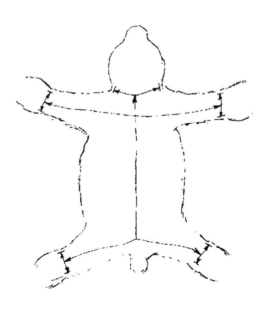

10 Into the Kitchen

In the offing is a memorable event at the dinner table, if the culinary mastery of the chef equals the field-handling abilities of the hunter.

10 Into the Kitchen

The hunter has done everything right, from the moment of kill. It's now up to the chef. At hand is the finest meat in the world. In the offing is a memorable event at the dinner table, if the culinary mastery of the chef equals the field-handling abilities of the hunter.

Once again, experience is the final teacher. And to get started right, or to reconsider methods used in the past, a few basic points should be borne in mind.

1. Most game meat has less fat distributed in the muscle fibers. It is important therefore to retain moisture during cooking. Stripping with bacon or brushing with melted fat will help. Larding is also useful for certain cuts. Bits of suet may be inserted; for this, there is nothing like a larding tool. The chef who lacks one should put off the purchase no longer.

2. The novice in game meat cookery almost always will overcook the meat. Perhaps the villain is a subconscious mistrust of game meat and a feeling that it's got to be far over on the well-done side to be tender.

3. Cook game for what it is. It does not need disguises.

4. Marinades, tenderizers, and seasonings enhance the tastes of domestic meats. The same is true of game. Mildly acid marination tenderizes meat. So do pounding and cooking under pressurized heat.

5. Game can be cooked by either dry heat or moist methods. Use dry heat for the tender cuts from younger animals, sirloin, ribs, chops, steaks. Prepare less tender cut with moist heat methods.

DRY HEAT methods include roasting, usually uncovered in a slow oven, 300-350 degrees, about twenty-five minutes per pound; broiling, either under broiler or over charcoal; pan broiling in a heavy frying pan rubbed with a small amount of suet.

MOIST HEAT methods include stewing and braising.

Mildly acid substances common to the kitchen are simple and effective marinades for game meat. These include vinegar, fruit juices, tomato juice, French dressing, and tomato sauce or undiluted tomato soup.

For a little more exotic marination, try one of the following:

1. 1/4 cup vinegar combined with 1/2 cup cooking oil, 1/2 teaspoon black pepper, 1/4 teaspoon garlic salt.

2. 2 cups vinegar, 2 cups water, 1/2 tablespoon sugar, 2 bay leaves, 1 teaspoon salt, 12 whole cloves, 1 teaspoon allspice, 3 medium sized onions sliced.

3. Blend equal parts of Worcestershire sauce and two of your favorite steak sauces, then add garlic salt, salt and pepper to taste.

4. 1/2 cup olive oil, 1/4 cup Chianti, 1 clove crushed garlic, 1/2 teaspoon black pepper, 1/8 teaspoon oregano, 1 teaspoon salt.

The ingredients in a marinade must always be thoroughly mixed and then stored in the refrigerator for several hours before using to permit blending of flavors. When ready for use, shake marinade well, use sufficient quantity to cover the meat, and allow meat to marinate twenty-four hours before broiling or roasting.

Keep in mind that game meat fat, especially venison, tends to congeal while still warm. For this reason, hot dishes should be served PIPING HOT.

11 *Onto the Table*

Game isn't called "game" without reason, and when the gamesmanship is tops from the firing of the gun to the carving of the haunch, the winning is without comparison.

11 | *Onto the Table*

Antlered animal meats, deer, moose, elk, pronghorn:

Roast American

Use a five-pound chunk of meat, rump, top of round, loin, or rib. Roll and tie if necessary. Lard generously with bits of suet. Salt and pepper to taste. Place meat in conventional roasting pan and roast in low oven, about 300 degrees, basting frequently with liquid shortening. Allow thirty-five minutes cooking time per pound. Carve across the grain of the meat. Serves six.

Spicy Roast

Mix: 2 cups water, 1 bay leaf, 1/8 teaspoon thyme, 1/8 teaspoon basil, 1/4 teaspoon crushed peppercorn, 1/2 teaspoon celery salt, 1/2 teaspoon salt.

Place a four-pound roast in a heavy pan and add the seasoning mixture. Cross the top of the roast with four slices of bacon. Cover pan. Simmer on top of stove until meat is tender. Before meat has finished cooking, diced, sliced, or quartered vegetables may be added, such as carrots, potatoes, onions, rutabagas. Add vegetables in plenty of time for them to cook to tenderness when roast is done. When

97

cooking is complete, add 1/2 cup sour cream, and if necessary reheat, but don't boil, and serve scalding hot. Serves six.

Sauerbrate

Mix: 5 cups vinegar, 5 cups water, 3 sliced onions, 1 sliced lemon, 12 whole cloves, 6 bay leaves, 6 whole pepper-corns, 3 tablespoons salt. Place six-pound rump roast in a large bowl, add mixture and let the meat stand thirty-six hours, turning occasionally. Remove meat and brown in hot fat. Add 1 cup of the seasoning mixture, cover tightly, and cook slowly until tender, adding a little water if necessary. Serves eight.

Barbeque

Mix: 1 cup catsup, 1 tablespoon salt, 2 tablespoons Worcestershire sauce, 1/4 cup vinegar, 1 tablespoon butter, 1/8 teaspoon cinnamon, 3 slices lemon, 1 thinly sliced onion, 1/8 teaspoon allspice.

Bring mixture to boil in a saucepan, stirring to avoid burning, and simmer for ten minutes.

While mixture is simmering, sear a three-pound roast on top of stove. Cover seared meat with sauce mixture and roast in a moderate oven, 350 degrees, for about two hours, turning the meat occasionally. Serves four to six.

Antlered Meat Vino

Cover a six-pound roast with a handful of rosemary. Set it on an open roaster rack and dribble a cup of melted butter over it. Add a cup of dry red wine to the bosom of the roasting pan. Roast in a 325-degree oven. When the wine has turned dark brown (but don't burn it) add a cup of water over the roast and baste frequently until the meat is brown and tender, adding a little more water as necessary. Allow thirty minutes to the pound—and don't get lazy with the basting.

Roast For Single And Guest

Pound 1/2 cup of flour into sides of a two-pound roast. Brown in 1/2 stick of butter. Add 4 teaspoons bacon fat, 1/2 teaspoon of salt, 1/4 teaspoon black pepper, 1 tablespoon chopped celery, 1 tablespoon chopped onion, 3/4 cup boiling water. Cover tightly and simmer for forty-five minutes. Add another 3/4 cup boiling water. Simmer until tender. Serve by candlelight.

Note to gravy lovers: strain the roast stocks, add necessary water, thicken to suit with flour, season to taste. The results make packaged gravy mixes obsolete.

Steaks, Chops, Cutlets, Loins From Antlered Animals

Charcoal or electric broil as you would a fine piece of beef. Or treat the cuts with the following recipes:

Garnished Broil

Brush steak or chop well with cooking oil. Sprinkle with garlic salt and place in broiler or over very hot charcoal. Sear and turn quickly several times to retain juices. Don't overcook. Meantime, have prepared: 1/2 teaspoon salt, 1/2 teaspoon pepper, 1 tablespoon chopped parsley mixed in 1/4 cup butter until creamy, then 1 1/2 tablespoons lemon added slowly. Spread piping hot chops with the mixture and garnish platter with parsley. The mixture may be made in advance and refrigerated. Mixture will spread about four medium-sized chops.

Sour Cream Cutlets

Roll a couple of two-pound steaks in a cup of flour, beating flour in slightly. Brown steaks quickly in very hot, but not burned, butter. With steaks in pan, add 1 cup sour cream, 1 bay leaf, 4 tablespoons butter, 2 teaspoons celery salt, 2 tablespoons Worcestershire sauce, fresh ground peppercorns to taste. Cover, bring to boil over high heat, then reduce heat and simmer until tender. Serves six.

Swiss Steak Madrid

Pound 1/2 cup flour into a round steak 1-inch thick. Sear the meat in 2 tablespoons of hot cooking oil. Add 1 cup canned tomatoes, 1 medium sized onion chopped, 1 green pepper chopped, 1/4 cup chopped celery, 2 teaspoons salt, 1/2 teaspoon pepper, and 2 tablespoons fat. Bring to boil, then reduce heat and simmer, covered, for about 1 1/2 hours.

Stews From Antlered Animals

Robin Hood Special

Cover the bottom of a large pan, or Dutch oven, with vegetable oil and get it hot. While the oil is heating, roll a pound of 1-inch cubes of meat in flour. Brown flouted meat in oil. Add 2 1/2 cups boiling water, 2 tablespoons chopped onion, 1/2 chopped garlic clove, 1 1/2 teaspoons salt, 1/2 teaspoon paprika, 1 teaspoon sugar, 1/2 tablespoon lemon juice, 1/2 tablespoon Worcestershire sauce, 1/4 cup tomato juice. Cover tightly and simmer two hours. Add a little more water if needed. Add 1 cup pearl onions, 1/2 cup diced celery, 1/2 cup diced carrots, 1 cup cubed potatoes and continue cooking until vegetables are done. Pour off juices and thicken to suit with a flour-water paste. Add gravy to meat and vegetables. Serves six.

Stew A Vin

Cube a pound of meat, roll it in flour, and brown in hot oil. In a pot put 1/2 pint white wine, 1/4 pint red wine, 1/2 teaspoon salt, 1 small bay leaf, 4 freshly ground peppercorns, 1 teaspoon parsley flakes. Bring mixture to almost-boil and put in the browned meat along with 8 diced onions, 8 small potatoes cubed, and 8 cubed tomatoes. Cover and simmer for three hours. Serve over wild rice, piping hot. Serves six.

Hunter's Stew

Flour and brown 1 pound of meat diced into 1-inch cubes. Add 3 cups boiling water, 1 tablespoon lemon juice, 2 tablespoons diced onion, 1 1/2 teaspoons salt, 1/2 garlic clove, 1 teaspoon sugar, 1/2 tablespoon vinegar. Cover tightly and simmer for two hours. Add 1/4 cup tomato juice, 1 cup cubed potatoes, and 1/2 cup each of diced celery, carrots, and turnips, if desired. Cook until vegetables are done. Thicken the stock by adding flour-water paste or milk. Serves six.

Antlered Animal Burger Meat

Ground elk, deer, moose, or pronghorn meat may be used exactly as ground beef for hamburger patties, charcoaled

100

hamburger steaks, meat loafs etc. Increase the moisture content by adding two or three ounces of ground suet to each pound of burger meat before cooking, blending the suet well into the meat.

Bear

Bear hams and shoulders may be cured in salt and cooked by methods associated with cured meats. Methods related to venison and beef work well with bear steaks and roasts. The same is true of bear stewing meat.

Even today deep-mountain dwellers in the Appalachia region may depend in some part on game meat to help fill the table. Those most knowledgeable offer these suggestions relevant to bear meat: 1. Be sure to trim excess fat. 2. Fresh bear meat may be tenderized and the taste "blanded" by parboiling with three large apples added to each quart of water. When the apples have cooked to the point of disintegration, the meat may be removed, seasoned, and baked. 3. Bear meat is not excessively dry, and dry heat cooking methods work well with it. 4. Serve bear meat well done. 5. The meat, even when well cooked, may have a pinkish tint when first sliced but will darken with exposure to air.

Lost Cove Roast

Sprinkle a four-pound roast with salt and pepper to taste and embed thin spears from two garlic cloves in the surface of the meat, scattering the spears in uniform distribution. Strip the top of the roast with four thin slices of bacon, anchoring them with toothpicks. Roast uncovered in 325-degree oven until tender. Serves eight.

Chops Parisien

Salt and pepper four chops and brown them in vegetable oil. Add a can of onion soup and a cup of water. Simmer for one hour. Serves four.

Bighorn Sheep

Cook as mutton.

Garlic is an especially good seasoning. Trim out all excess fat before cooking.

Bighorn Curry

Brown two pounds lean, cubed meat in 2 tablespoons hot fat. Cover with boiling water and add salt and pepper to taste, crushed garlic clove, 1 bay leaf, 6 whole peppercorns, 1 teaspoon chopped parsley, 2 small onions. Cover and cook slowly two hours or until meat is tender. Strain stock and reserve 2 cups. Mix 1/4 cup of flour with 1 teaspoon curry powder, adding 2 tablespoons cold water to make a smooth paste. Stir the paste into stock and cook until thick. Add meat mixture. Serve with fluffy steamed rice. Serves six.

Pepper Chops

Brown six thick chops in hot fat and season to taste with salt and pepper. Place in baking pan. Cut six slices each from a green pepper, a medium-sized onion, and lemon. Top each chop with a slice of pepper, onion, and lemon. Pour 2 cups tomato juice over the garnished chops. Cover and bake in 325-degree oven about 1 1/2 hours. Serves six.

Boar (Wild Hog)

Wild hog may be fried, roasted, or barbecued with methods applicable to domestic pork.

In addition to tabling wild hog prepared from your favorite pork recipes, try these taste-bud treats:

Ham and Redeye

Slicing across the grain of the meat, take quarter-inch-thick center cuts from a ham that's been cured and then smoked to a rich amber color. Use about a pound of meat for three or four servings. Preheat a frying pan (a heavy cast-iron skillet is preferable) and wipe it inside with a piece of pork fat. Rinse the center cuts first in warm water and then very cold water. Sponge the meat dry and place it in the hot skillet so that the meat edges don't overlap. Turn it after a couple of minutes, searing each side. Reduce heat to low medium and fry it well done. (Until the fat around the edges has darkened and got the slightest bit brittle.) While the meat is still in the skillet, mix 1/4 cup water with 3/8 cup black, perked coffee. Pour the liquid in with the meat, cover quickly and let it simmer for five minutes. Serve the redeye gravy in

102

a nest of stiffly cooked grits or with hot biscuits.

Sausage

Because of its fat content, artificial seasonings, and methods of mass preparation, most commercial pork sausage is a poor echo of the real thing. The preparation of sausage in the home permits use of lean portions, rather than scraps and trimmings. The chef lucky enough to have access to wild hog meat does it this way:

Take ten pounds of very lean meat, such as tenderloin. Chop it (don't grind it!) into very small pieces, about the size of medium green peas. Put the meat into a large wooden bowl and add 1/4 cup salt, 1/8 cup dark brown sugar, 2 tablespoons sage, 2 teaspoons each of black and red pepper. Stir the meat and seasonings until everything is evenly distributed. Then beat the mixture with a wooden mallet or wooden steak beater until the seasonings and meat are thoroughly blended. Refrigerate sausage for forty-eight hours before shaping into patties and frying. The sausage may be stored in several ways: Shape into patties and freeze; pack it in small cloth bags and smoke it for a week; form into balls, pack in a crockery jar, cover with boiling grease, cover jar with a loose cheesecloth to keep out insects, and store in a dim, cool place.

Opossum

Yammy Possum

In the South, this meat is most commonly associated with yams. To prepare the one-time staple on rural Southern tables, parboil the cleaned and readied carcass, either whole or in pieces, in water containing salt and red pepper to taste. When the meat is tender, place in a lightly greased pan and surround it with quartered yams. Bake until golden brown in a 300-degree oven.

Possum Sassafras

Prepare in exactly the same way that **Yam Possum** is

cooked, except omit greasing of baking pan. Instead, line the bottom of the pan with sassafras sticks.

Fried

Divide the carcass into small pieces and parboil in salty water until tender. Then salt and red pepper to taste, roll in flour, and fry in hot fat.

Rabbit

Fried

There are two popular methods of frying rabbit. In each the rabbit is sectioned into pieces with the legs removed and the ribs and back separated, older rabbits being parboiled in salty water to tenderize.

1. Salt and pepper to taste and put the pieces in a greased pan, frying until golden brown.

2. Make a batter with two eggs, 4 tablespoons flour, 1/4 cup milk, and 1/2 teaspoon pepper. Salt to taste. Dip salted pieces in batter and drop into very hot fat to deep fry. (The battered pieces may also be baked until golden brown, about thirty minutes.)

Mock Chicken Salad

Using favorite recipe for chicken salad, substitute rabbit for the chicken meat—and real chicken salad will be a come-down.

Rabbit Carolina

Put rabbit in a pot and cover it with water. Add 1 teaspoon of salt and stew rabbit until tender. Drain. Save the broth. Bone the rabbit and cut the meat into coarse chunks. Melt 1/8 pound of butter in a large frying pan and add 1 cup diced potatoes, 1/2 cup diced celery, 1/2 cup diced carrots, and 1 medium-sized onion sliced. Add just enough water to keep ingredients from scorching, then cover and cook for fifteen minutes. Add 2 cups of broth and an eight ounce can of tomato sauce. Bring to a boil. Put in the rabbit meat, 1/2 cup chopped parsley, 1/4 cup flour, and salt to taste. Simmer for a final fifteen minutes. Serves four.

Bunny Vin

Prepare a marinade by heating, just to the boiling point, a mixture of 1 cup water, 1 cup plain table wine, and 4 tablespoons olive oil. Place pieces of rabbit in earthenware jar and cover with two medium-sized onions sliced, 1 teaspoon salt, 1/4 teaspoon black pepper, and 1/4 teaspoon oregano. Now pour in the heated, liquid mixture until the meat is covered. Cap the container and let rabbit marinate in the refrigerator for two days. Strain the marinade and dry the meat. Brown the meat in hot fat and then lay the meat in a casserole. Estimate the amount of strained marinade it will take to cover the meat in the casserole. Heat this amount in the pan in which the rabbit was browned, thereby including juices left in the pan. Pour the heated liquid over the rabbit meat, cover the casserole, and cook with low heat for forty minutes. Serve over noodles.

Spitted Rabbit (or any other kind of game meat)

Make a baste of a handful of chopped parsley, two crushed cloves of garlic, half a dozen freshly ground peppercorns, and 1/2 cup of olive oil. Spit meat and cook before open flame, not close enough to scorch surface without getting inner meat done, turning meat so that juices are sealed in. Swab frequently with basting mix and salt to taste when done.

Raccoon

If the coon carcass was carelessly or ineptly handled in the field, don't bother to cook the meat. It will be too strong for human consumption.

Coon illustrates the effects of field handling with a clarity that should jar the most lethargic attitude. While the coon carcass is particularly sensitive, the same processes begin in all meats at the moment of kill. Coon is the object lesson in field handling well worth remembering when any variety of game is felled.

If the coon carcass was properly handled (bled, cooled, deglanded, skinned without the hair contaminating the meat, etc.) the cook has excellent meat with which to work.

First: Remove excess fat, including that between the muscle bands. The fat has an objectionable taste and odor. To enhance the taste, try parboiling the meat in water containing several broken spicewood twigs, or a large onion, or a teaspoon of vinegar, or two or three whole Irish potatoes, peeled.

Golden Coon

Parboil to tender with 1 teaspoon of salt per pound of meat, 1 pod of red pepper, 1 tablespoon black pepper, and spicewood twigs added to water. Remove meat and pat off excess moisture. Arrange pieces in a baking pan rubbed lightly with vegetable oil and bake until golden brown at 325 degrees.

Southern Fry

Parboil as with Golden Coon, roll pieces of meat in cornmeal and deep fry in very hot fat.

Coon Supreme

Halve the treated and readied carcass into two sides, not fore and hindquarters. Parboil. Place on rack in a baking pan. Prepare a baste of 1/2 cup vegetable oil, 1 1/2 teaspoons sage, 1 clove crushed-garlic. Baste the coon sides often while baking them until tender in a 350-degree oven.

Coon Delight

Mix: 2 cups coon meat, minced after cooking, 1 cup chopped celery, 1 1/4 teaspoon salt, 3 freshly ground peppercorns, 2 tablespoons each of chopped green pepper and chopped parsley, 1/3 cup mayonnaise, 1 teaspoon vegetable oil. Use the delight for sandwiches, serve as a salad in lettuce nests, or for hors d'oeuvres.

Squirrel

Millions of squirrels have been eaten, and members of the loyal order of squirrel meat fanciers rarely desert the ranks.

'Bama Fry

First timers should start off with fried squirrel. Just salt the pieces to taste, add a dash of black pepper, roll the meat in flour, and drop it into hot fat.

Squirrel Dusseldorf

Season and brown pieces of meat in hot fat. Arrange pieces on the bottom of a sufficiently large pot. Open a can of sauerkraut large enough to cover the squirrel in a fairly thick layer. Add 1/2 cup water and sprinkle very sparingly with caraway seed. Cover tightly and simmer until meat is tender. A pressure cooker may be substituted for the pot. If so, cooking time is about twenty minutes.

Squirrel and Mushrooms

Salt and pepper pieces of meat from one squirrel to taste. Roll in flour and brown in skillet. Place in baking dish and add 1/2 cup each of chopped celery and chopped onions, 1 cup mushroom buttons, 1/2 cup milk, 1/2 cup cream. Cover and bake at 350 degrees until tender.

Grandma's Dumplings

Make up your favorite dumpling mix, basing the quantity on 1 cup flour.

Place squirrel pieces in a large pot, add salt to taste and a generous dash or two of black pepper. Cover with hot water and simmer until meat is tender. Drop in dumplings, cover, and cook ten minutes. Then add one cup of milk in which a tablespoon of flour has been dissolved.

Woodchuck

The best chuck is taken between early September and hibernation time. The animals at that period are at prime.

Fry

Disjoint and divide the carcass into convenient pieces. Boil until tender in moderately salted water to which has been added a tablespoon of vinegar. Remove the meat, pat off excess moisture, and then flour the meat, working the flour in well. Deep fry in hot fat until brown. Finish salting to taste.

Yankee Chuck

Salt and pepper pieces of chuck to taste. Roll in flour. Put 1/4 cup, or a little less, of vegetable oil in a baking pan. Place

107

meat in greased pan and bake uncovered until golden. Use a 350-degree oven. When meat has browned, add just enough water to cover with 1 chopped garlic clove in the water. Simmer slowly until water evaporates.

Exotic Burgers

Strip the meat raw from the bones of one woodchuck. Grind the meat. Mix the meat with 1/2 cup bread crumbs, 1/4 cup ground onion, 1 teaspoon salt, 1/8 teaspoon pepper, 1 beaten egg, 1 tablespoon melted fat. Shape into patties. Dip patties in a batter made with 1 beaten egg and 1/2 cup cracker meal. Fry to brown in hot fat. Then place in casserole, cover each patty lightly with currant jelly sauce and bake in a 300-degree oven for about an hour.

Game Birds

Fine hotel chefs remind us that quail, grouse, partridge, and similar game birds should be barded, that is, stripped with bacon for cooking.

Roast Whole Quail

Season six birds outside and inside with salt and pepper to taste. Roll birds in a roasting pan containing a "skin" of melted butter. Place birds on backs and bard with strips of bacon. Roast in 500-degree oven for fifteen minutes. Reduce heat to 350 degrees and continue roasting until tender, basting often with butter. Serves six.

Fried Quail

Have on hand one quail per serving. Split each bird down the back, leaving the breasts intact. Flatten each bird, breast down. Sprinkle with salt to taste. Shake each bird in a paper bag containing 1/2 cup flour. Fry breast down in skillet containing enough very hot lard to cover birds halfway up. Turn when breast is golden and continue hot-fry until birds are golden all over, turning often to keep from scorching any spots. Turn down heat, cover, and continue as with frying chicken. Birds will be tender in about thirty minutes cooking time. Remove to drain rack and sprinkle lightly with paprika.

Use portion of residue in the pan to make desired amount of cream gravy.

Quail Fricassee

Fry the grease out of six slices of bacon. Remove bacon. Cut the birds in half, season with salt and pepper, and lay them in the hot grease. Sprinkle lightly with grated onion and flour. When birds are browned on one side, turn and lightly sprinkle with flour, omitting onion. Add water sufficient to simmer, cover, and simmer until tender.

Quail Sherry

Salt and pepper six quail and place them in a large casserole with 1 sprig of parsley, 1 small bay leaf, 1 pint of soup stock, 1 medium-sized whole onion. Cover and bake at 400 degrees for 1/2 hour, then reduce heat to 350 degrees and continue baking until birds are tender. Remove casserole from oven. In a separate pan heat 1 tablespoon butter, add 1 tablespoon flour, stirring. When butter-flour mixture is brown add the sauce from the birds. Bring to boil and remove from heat, adding 1 cup button mushrooms, cooked, 1 tablespoon catsup, and 1/2 cup sherry. Pour the sauce all over the birds, return casserole to oven. When piping hot, serve.

Broiled Pheasant

Split the bird down the middle, salt, pepper, and rub it all over with sweet cream butter. Wrap with hickory-smoked bacon and broil close to flame. When bacon has browned, reduce flame until bird is done to taste. Baste frequently with bacon and butter drippings from the bottom of the broiling pan.

Pheasant With Cream

Soak three or four cut-up pheasants for three hours in enough water to cover which contains 1 teaspoon soda and 1 tablespoon of salt. Dry the meat, season lightly with salt and pepper, and roll in flour. Brown in hot fat. Then put the pieces in a Dutch oven, add 2 tablespoons of water to the frying pan containing the browning residue and pour con-

109

tents of the browning pan over the pheasant. Add 1/2 pint of cream, cover, and bake at 300 degrees for about three hours.

Roast Wild Duck

Fill cavity of duck with 2 medium-sized apples quartered and peeled. Stitch cavity closed. Rub with a slice of onion. Salt and pepper, for an average dressed duck (about 1 1/2 pounds) using 2 teaspoons salt and 1/4 teaspoon pepper. Roast uncovered in 325-degree oven, twenty to thirty minutes per pound. During cooking, baste every ten minutes with small amounts of orange juice.

Wisconsin Duck

Ready as for roasting. Surround duck in roasting pan with 2 peeled and quartered apples, sweetening if tart, and sauerkraut. A little water may be added if needed. Bake until browned at 325 degrees.

Duck A La Mode

Cut into serving pieces. Salt and pepper and roll in flour. In a deep, heavy skillet, heat 1/4 cup butter. Brown the meat. Sprinkle with 1/2 teaspoon thyme and add 1 cup heavy cream. Cover and simmer over low heat about 1 1/2 hours, until tender.

Roast Wild Turkey

Boil giblets until tender. Skin and chop fine. Combine with 2 quarts minced stale bread, 1 large finely chopped onion, 1 cup of raisins, 2 non-tart apples diced. Mix and add salt, pepper, and minced garlic to taste. Moisten and stuff turkey, closing the cavity with skewers and twine. Place turkey in roasting pan and brush 2 tablespoons melted butter onto bird, then sprinkle lightly with flour. Put 1 cup of water in roasting pan and roast in 350-degree oven about twenty minutes per pound, basting often.

Turkey Papil

Take a clean paper sack large enough to fit comfortably over the bird and grease the sack inside with vegetable oil. Brush turkey with oil and salt and pepper well. Make your favorite basic poultry dressing and add oysters or button mushrooms, and stuff the bird. Close the body cavity and put the bird inside the brown paper bag, making certain the bag doesn't crush down and touch the bird except on the back. Twist the open end of the bag closed and tie it with a string. Put bagged bird in roasting pan and cook in a 325 degree oven for about twenty-five minutes per pound. When removed from oven, do not open the bag for twenty minutes, permitting the bird to steam.

Turkey On A Spit (Or any other land fowl)

Split the bird into two sides. Rinse with sherry. Melt enough butter to rub each side generously. Add salt and pepper to taste and a touch of thyme to melted butter. Rub bird well with butter mixture, then spit each side and roast slowly turning birds to desired doneness, depending on size. Baste frequently with a half-and-half mixture of the melted butter and sherry.

Roast Wild Goose

The old standby, known to most cooks, is hard to beat:

Stuff a goose with non-tart apples, close the body cavity, salt and pepper to taste, and roast in a very hot oven for twenty minutes, then reduce to moderate heat and roast until tender, basting frequently with the drippings.

Goose Erin

Prepare a stuffing of 10 medium-sized potatoes boiled and diced, 1 tablespoon melted butter, 1 cup chopped onions, 1/2 cup chopped celery, 1/4 teaspoon pepper, 4 slices bread crumbled, 1/2 pound ground salt pork, 2 beaten eggs, 1 teaspoon poultry seasoning, and 1 teaspoon salt. (Save water in which potatoes boiled for basting.) Salt inside and outside of bird to taste, stuff with the stuffing mixture, close the body cavity, and roast in a 325-degree oven, basting now and then with potato water.

Royal Goose

Prepare a stuffing of cooked and minced giblets, 3 quarts of stale bread crumbled, 2 large minced garlic cloves, 1 large minced onion, 1/2 teaspoon ground oregano, 1 teaspoon ground sage, salt and pepper to taste. Moisten stuffing

111

ingredients with giblet stock and mix well. Rub inside of bird lightly with butter. Salt and pepper inside and outside of bird to taste. Stuff the bird and close the body cavity, with skewers or twine. Lightly rub outside of bird with butter and then sprinkle very lightly with flour. Roast covered bird at 325 degrees for about a half-hour per pound, until tender. Remove roaster cover for last few minutes of roasting time.

Ruffed Grouse (Partridge)
Prairie Chicken
Woodcock
Sharptail Grouse

Due to unusual similarity in preparation, these birds are grouped together. Many cooks use only the breasts of these birds, but the entire bird may be utilized.

Research turned up nothing finer than the following recipes and cooking methods for these birds, and they are offered courtesy of the foods and nutrition department, Michigan State University, via that state's wildlife division.

Broil

Open bird on back. If not tender, place in a small baking pan with 1/2 inch water, cover, and put in hot oven for fifteen minutes. Roll in flour and lay on broiling irons, breast down. Make gravy of 2 tablespoons flour in cold water, with pepper, salt, and butter. Stir in the liquid in which birds were parboiled. Use this gravy to serve with birds when they have broiled done. Serve also with bacon and toast, if preferred. Or slash birds in breast three times when done, put a little butter, salt, and pepper in each slash, place on toast, then pour liquid from pan over them.

Casserole

Cut birds into serving pieces and dip into milk, then flour. Fry until brown, salt to taste, put into casserole and cover with sour or sweet cream. Bake at 350 degrees until tender.

Roast

Prepare as for broiling. Place in dripping pan with 1 tablespoon butter. Bake at 450 degrees for five minutes, then reduce heat to 325 degrees and bake fifteen to twenty-five minutes longer, depending on size of bird. Baste frequently with drippings, salt and pepper to taste.

Remember that almost all recipes for domestic meat work well with game meat of similar texture, provided the game has been properly handled in the field. Also, try wild game recipes with your favorite cuts of domestic meats. And don't be afraid to shift a game meat recipe from one variety to another. Imagination and a little experimentation often help in turning out delightful dishes.

Remember also that game meat is the greatest for kabobs.

Game isn't called "game" without reason, and when the gamesmanship is tops from the firing of the gun to the carving of the haunch, the winning is without comparison.

12 *The Campfire Hour*

Wisdom, in the modern hunter, is revealed in the target chosen, in the respect and care with which the trigger is squeezed, in the way the field handling is conducted, and in the way you treat the environment and relate to wildlife ecology so that hunting will be even more rewarding in the next-generation day.

12 | *The Campfire Hour*

Hasn't it been a wonderful day? A golden, crisp, autumn dawn gently awakening the woodlands, the fading of mists from the valleys, the taste of air touched only by the kiss of wildflower and pine, the loamy path through sun-and-shade-dappled glen, the invitation by a pure spring bursting from a shaded, vine-trellised crevice to drink deeply, the racing creek spilling like diamonds over mossy stones and gurgling on through canopies of laurel and rhododendron.

The spoor has led the experienced tracker through the blazing fall colors of a wooded hillside, beyond the creek, across the slope of shale as the sun stands at zenith, down to a long meadow of sage and grass where insects hum lazily and the quarry browses, without antlers, barely beyond the age of fawnhood. The figure in khaki fatigues eases away, leaving the silence undisturbed, looking for fresh game sign.

Now, the crimson fire of sunset in the west, the hunter is closing his day, contented, relaxed, the coolness in gently creeping night shadows touching his brow, inviting peace. The campfire dances on its hearth of stones, and the quietude is broken by a sizzling drip from the wild turkey on its spit.

From Bullet to Table

For a few hours, lung-rattling smog, push-shove of cities, street gangs, AIDS epidemic, slaughter in the Balkans, starvation in Africa, governmental gridlock are realities a world away.

There is a sense of oneness with nature, a stirring in some recess of ancestral memories of the primeval hour when earth was the mother in a very real sense and the heavens declared the glory of the mystery of creation.

The day of the hunter. The experience unique.

Without those first hunters the human race would never have amounted to very much. Perhaps its brief appearance would today be recorded in fossilized stone. At best, if the hunter had never appeared, the race in scanty numbers would exist in those small environmental pockets where wild vegetation may sustain human life at subsistence level, as evidenced by the minuscule enclaves discovered in the Australian outback, the Kalahari region of Africa. Only the hunting tribes possessed the life-mode necessary to the spread, and survival, of mankind into hostile environments, over the entire landscape of the planet.

They appeared to have little going for them, that early *homo sapiens*. They were themselves possible meals for the predator endowed with fangs and claws.

But beneath the superficial appearance of helpless nakedness lurked traits and qualities that would prove the uniqueness of the breed. Whether you prefer to believe, while you search for a missing link, that the attributes evolved, or you choose to attribute the attributes to a power of creation doesn't alter the facts: The creature stood fully erect, its upper limbs detailed like none other. It could swim and climb. Its stamina over long distances was unparalleled. It could endure extremes of temperature. These were potential assets which required development and extension if they were to serve the creature well. Otherwise, the creature was confined to the immediate food source, and in periods of long-drawn drought it grubbed the final roots from the earth, weakened, and died.

The physical design included a mysterious, gray, wet lump set atop the upper extremity of the spine and encased in a protective armor of hemispheric bone with the hardness of stone but more resilient and shock-absorbent.

A process called thought took place in the gray lump called the brain, and even though the first desperate throwing of a stone or snatching up a tree limb to ward off a predator might have occurred as an animal-reflex, the next time it was by conscious memory, thought, and will.

It was the discovery of weaponry, by the brain atypical of all other species, the brain capable of analysis, of learning, of consciously applying what has been learned. The brain devised ways of throwing the stone farther, of shaping and balancing the club for greater effectiveness. The brain reasoned a fore-end sharpening of the thrown stick so that it penetrated a target, and a milestone brain envisioned a bow to speed and add range to a sharpened stick. A genius IQ feathered the arrow, endowing it with a predictable flight pattern.

But refinements were gradual, tedious, spread over many centuries, and the first hunter, carrying responsibility for the survival of the family, clan, tribe, had scant assurance of a successful return to the cave.

It followed that the most successful hunter was the natural leader. He assumed leadership and the tribe accepted; he planned the hunts and gave the orders. And the first primitive social order was created and emplaced.

When drought, earthquake, fire, flood, pestilence depleted a food supply, the hunting tribes survived, migrating, moving on, finding furred and feathered food whatever the climate. The bird, cattle, fish taken in an equatorial location might vary superficially in structure and color from the one in a distant arctic region. But the nutrients, including those by-passed by the vegetarian, were equally life-sustaining.

Following signs of game, the migrants arrive at its source, the plain or valley or mountainside teeming with game. But previous migrants are already there, claiming the territory.

And so the hunter-leader becomes the warrior king, devising the strategy, in the van as the previous claimants are driven out. As warrior-king he has the further responsibility of defending the territory from invasion by hungry strangers.

This early humankind revealed its priorities in drawings and scratchings on the walls of sheltering caves. We see the primitive bison and giant tiger as human eyes and hands recorded them. We share the experience of a tribe hounding a woolly mammoth to exhaustion in preparation for the final attack. It was attack from all sides by women as well as men. It was extremely dangerous, this use of lances and stone-headed clubs against the enraged behemoth. It exacted a toll in injuries and sometimes a human life. When it was over, nothing was wasted, from hide and hair to the smallest needle-sized bone. And the hunt was told at the campfire, and the tellings became traditions, and tribes waxed strong in the acts of living up to their traditions.

The brain of the creature was constantly noting and storing data, and, all-importantly, putting it to use.

He noted that wood which a fire had not entirely consumed was harder than normal. From then on, he processed his sharpened sticks in the flames.

As he learned the uses of flint during passing millennia and ways of napping it to razor sharpness, the fire-hardened stick was outmoded. The flint-headed stick became state of the art, in the form of arrow, spear, lance.

Having devised the bow, he sought the most resilient wood and flexible, toughest tendon to make the weapon.

He domesticated the wolf and made it his servant-partner.

He devised the deadfall. And as the art of weaving grasses, reeds, and strips of bark and wood came into being, he fashioned fish traps and nets. The remarkable brain put the net to multiple uses. With it, the hunter took food from the rivers, lakes, even the seas. He stretched it over game trails and lurked in the lower tree branches to drop it over a passing animal. He deployed it across the trail and beat the bush so that frightened animals stampeded into the net.

He envisioned a boar restricted in a hole, and he dug a pit and camouflaged it with brush. And if the boar didn't cooperate by wandering along and falling in, the hunter went out, located a boar, and lured him into charging. If the boar didn't charge straight-on as he was supposed to or the brush cover didn't break and send him crashing into the depths, the wise hunter had a tree already picked to climb with an agility surpassed only by the apes.

The cleverness and daring and sheer determination of the earliest hunters reflect across the millennia, persisting in certain areas into the modern era.

The plains Indian of North America who followed the great herds of bison is well known to everyone. The day by day lifestyle was nomadic, and the hour of hunt was fraught with risks, being caught in the path of wheeling, stampeding buffalo, a goring by a desperate animal singled out for the kill. When the hunt had produced a sufficiency, a temporary camp was set up to serve as abattoir and processing plant. Everyone shared the duties, the dressing of hides, the stripping of meat for dry-curing, the excising of tendons for thread, lacing, rope, the cleaning of bones which were raw material in the making of mallets, needles, awls.

Lesser known is the basic tactic of the small tribe once roaming the area that is present-day Arizona-New Mexico. A small group of hunters would target a wild horse and, quite simply, run him to death. Beginning the chase, the hunters appeared to be hopelessly outclassed, but each time the horse had drawn sufficiently far ahead to pause for breath he had to continue because the hunters were always there, trotting tirelessly, closing the distance. Each time the gaps shortened. Finally the horse's forelegs buckled.

In the Ituri region of Africa, in the time when the rhino moved in great numbers, a pygmy people akin to the Akka, averaging less than four-feet in individual height, were observed in their hunts by white explorers.

The diminutive hunters would station themselves singly

against stout trees near a grazing rhino. When everyone was in place a hand signal from the leader was given. A lone warrior would set up hue-cry-shouting, jumping up and down, making threatening feints and gestures. When the rhino got the message and charged, the pygmy stood his ground until the final second. With the fiery breath of the enormous beast spewing at his face, the tiny hunter in a flash ducked behind his tree. The near-sighted rhino, intent upon his enemy, crashed full tilt into the tree. As the tree shuddered and the dazed rhino staggered back, a hunter at a tree across the way took his turn attracting the rhino's attention. Perhaps the tiny brain of the gigantic beast mistook the hunter as the previous one, charging ever more furiously. The little fellows beguiled the frustrated brute from tree crash to tree crash, until the exhausted, half-conscious rhino was pared down to size, at which moment the hunters descended on him.

The pygmy who could hardly dent the string in an English longbow still managed to bring down the elephant with his arrow. In his rain forest the clever hunter would first fashion a sizeable sack from barkcloth. He hadn't far to go to find a nest of poisonous fire ants. The leader and the bravest of his lieutenants would dig up the nest, filling the sack with the roiling mass. Tied securely at the mouth and hung on a tree branch, the contents of the sack rapidly metamorphosed in the steaming jungle, becoming a deadly poisonous, sticky substance. Into this the pygmy dipped an arrow that was hardly more than a dart compared to the missile of a Viking. But few Vikings killed elephantine creatures more efficiently. The pygmy hunter simply penetrated the tough hide with two or three of his arrows. To an elephant, mere pricks. To the pygmy, occasion to break glorious news to the tribe. To the tribe, the promise of a gala as they followed the lumbering beast at a safe distance until the moment arrived when the poison had done its work and the elephant keeled over.

All peoples are endowed with inventive wit. Oft-times it flourishes most heartily in most adverse environmental circumstance. The spectral alternative to survival is powerful motivation indeed.

Few of us have had to respond to conditions facing the pygmy—nor the early Eskimo living north of the Arctic Circle. The pygmy could not envision the Eskimo, nor the Eskimo the pygmy. They lived in environments so unlike that they might have belonged to separate planets. But undoubtedly, had they been able to view each other, they would have felt a kinship as members of the brotherhood of hunters, esteeming boldness, courage, and ingenuity wherever found.

Each would have marvelled at the other's feats, and neither, it's more than probable, would have wanted to exchange places, the pygmy from his nicely hot and humid forest to the barren wastes of ice where not even a grass grew, the Eskimo to the sweltering, smothering green of a weird forest filled with vines and creepers, scuttling lizards and slithering poisonous snakes. The Eskimo would return to his twilight Arctic noon to tell about the strange little black man who hunted a beast rivalling the whale in size. He would marvel at the pygmy while taking his own marvels for granted. Even as he narrated his spell-binding tale, cross-ankled, the center of attention at a campfire, the Eskimo's hands would be busy fashioning the key weapon for his next hunt. In the history of weaponry, few devices have reflected more cleverness.

First the Eskimo chose a piece of resilient whalebone and cut it into a long, narrow strip. He scraped the strip almost paper thin. He then sharpened all the edges until any would sever a hair from the cheek. He rolled the strip tightly and tied it with a tendon cord. He inserted the small cylinder of coiled whalebone in a piece of whale or seal meat, and mushed his lightly laden sled and dog team north, toward the wan rim of an almost non-existent sun.

When he cut and read polar bear sign, he tossed his frozen bait on the crust of white ice that comprised the world from horizon to horizon. Then he moved aside, to a deeper darkness beneath a sheltering drift, to wait in infinite patience.

He watched the white shadow of the denizen of the

123

twilight world as it shuffled to the bait and nuzzled. He saw the polar bear gulp the irresistible morsel. As the huge white mass of muscle power, so easily aroused to blind ferocity, plodded onward, the Eskimo stirred his dogs.

He followed the bear at a distance. He didn't keep track of the hours. At fifty degrees below zero, time itself may be measured only by the coming and going of the howling gale winds whipping curtains of snow across the frozen landscape.

He followed the bear's tracks through one meal time, and the next, and the one after that. The marks of disturbance in the snow told him where the bear's digestive juices had dissolved the piece of seal meat and the tendon that bound the whalebone cylinder.

He mused a moment, thinking of the inner tearing as the tightly coiled whalebone cylinder flashed to its full length, ripping and cutting through stomach fibers. He thanked the spirit of the great bear and continued the path marked by the huge-paw tracks. He hung tenaciously to the trail beneath a sky of darkness, on a surface of blinding white while an alien world beyond a horizon of black-on-white marked its scurrying hours as morning, noon, night, numbers on the faces of its clocks.

He followed until he ran out of food for both himself and his dogs. And he would not stop, wondering at this most marvelous and god-like of polar bears.

When finally he came to the end where the great bear lay, he paused at last, paying a final homage, thanking the king of beasts, and patiently quartering for loading onto the sled the source of survival for himself and his family in the immediate days ahead, when he would set out to hunt the seal if they were running.

Who knows when and how the first Eskimo was lured toward the wastelands centered by the north pole? Who were the Elamites prior to evidences they left of themselves in the mid-East? Where did they come from?

Events occurring after the invention of writing we can summarize more clearly and accurately, and in some cases of earlier people-movement we can answer questions from fossils and archeological findings. Whatever the case, we can make one assumption with surety: The hunter was always in the vanguard, at movement point. When Eric The Red made landfall on Greenland, it was the hunter/warrior who stepped ashore.

The spread of the United States from ocean to ocean followed the trails marked by the first hunters. The planned mapping expeditions of Lewis and Clarke, as well as countless others, relied on its hunters to provide the greater part of the food supply. The same was true of wagon trains pushing the frontier always westward. And the analogy is applicable without exception, from the movement of Mongol hordes across a continent to the landing on an unknown Pacific island by Bora-Borans.

The hunter was the scout, finding the passage through the mountains, the water hole in the desert, whatever the language he spoke

Primitive hunts, as we've mentioned, were often family affairs. Women's acts of courage, their prowess in the chase, frequently exceeded that of the men, especially if the children were threatened. Their exploits were told by tellers of tales and sung poetically at campfires, so much so that in time they joined the mythological pantheons as goddesses of the hunt. The two most familiar to us are Diana and Artemis, Roman and Greek names for the goddess of the hunt. In ancient cultures, priestesses of the hunt goddess were revered as having mystical powers; in some cities the main temple was dedicated to the hunt goddess.

One of the oldest accounts of a woman huntress is that of Atalanta, whose name reminds us of an ocean. It would have been more fitting to name a land of the most ferocious lions, tigers, wild bulls, and killer gorillas after her. She would have flicked the hem of her tunic at the lot of them.

Her story is told in full by Ovid and Apollodorus, but it is

125

certain that they based their accounts on tales first told far before their times.

She started life as an abandoned baby. Seems her father had wanted a son so fervently he could not accept the fact that a daughter had been born. He left the tiny creature on a wild mountainside, where she assuredly would die of cold and hunger. But a she-bear found the infant, took her to her den, nursed her, and kept her warm.

The babe survived and grew into active, daring girlhood. Kind hunters crossed her path about this time and invited her to join them. Living with them, she learned all the arduous modes of a hunter's life.

Only the nymphs rivaled her in loveliness, and many stricken, swooning swains would have paid with his life at sunup for a night with her. However, mere men did not interest her all that much.

Her superhuman courage was evident early on. It was put to full test by two centaurs who caught sight of her when she was alone. These fearsome monsters had the heads and torsos of men and the bodies of war horses. Anything mortal had little chance against them in conflict.

They chased after Atalanta, who, hearing the thunderous hoofbeats, turned to face them. She refused to run or beg for mercy. Instead, quite coolly, she fitted an arrow to her bow and shot one centaur dead. Seeing this, the second came on in heightened fury. Atalanta had but a few moments to fit a second arrow. Her aim was perfect. The arrow flew to its mark and the remaining centaur fell dead, also.

Her most famous exploit occurred when she joined in the hunt for the Calydonian boar. This was a fearsome creature only the mind of an insulted goddess could have dreamed up. The goddess was Artemis, in extremely high dudgeon because Oeneus, the mortal king of Calydon, had neglected her when he sacrificed first-fruits to the gods at harvest time.

As punishment, Artemis sent her terrible creature to

ravage the land of Calydon. The brute devastated the countryside, destroying cattle, and killing the bravest and hardiest of men sent to kill it. Finally, in desperation Oeneus called upon all Greece to send its finest hunters to help him. A splendid band of young heroes assembled. As a matter of course Atalanta, "The Pride of the Woods of Arcady," appeared among the company.

A Greek writer gives an intriguing description of her: "A shining buckle clasped her robe at the neck; her hair was simply dressed, caught in a bun behind. An ivory quiver hung upon her left shoulder and in her hand was a bow. Thus was she attired. As for her face it was too maidenly to be that of a boy."

Oeneus's son, Meleager, fell in love with her at first sight. She was the loveliest and most desirable maiden he had ever seen, but Atalanta preferred to treat him as a good hunting companion.

When the company found and surrounded the terrible boar, it charged them so swiftly that two men were killed in the blink of an eye. It raged everywhere. In the noise and confusion of wildly flying weapons and dying men, Atalanta kept her head,

She fitted an arrow and wounded the monster so grievously Meleager was able to rush upon it and stab it through the heart.

The boar hunt had a most tragic ending. Though he had technically killed the boar, Meleager insisted that the skin go to Atalanta. This enraged two of his uncles, his mother's brothers, and Meleager, taking preventive defensive action, caught them off guard and killed them. Whereupon, Meleager's mother, Althea, hearing the news, was seized by a passion of rage.

Her beloved brothers had been slain by her son because he had made a fool of himself over a shameless hussy. She released a curse whereby Meleager fell to the ground dying.

As his spirit slipped away from his body, Althea was horror-stricken by what she had done and hanged herself.

Atalanta was far from the ending of her adventures. As she came to the full bloom of womanhood she was so beset by swains who wanted her that she finally haughtily said she would marry the man who could beat her in a footrace. None came close, until Melanion beheld her, and wanted her more than anything else the world had to offer.

Unlike his predecessors, Melanion used his head to enhance his physical powers. By the favor of Aphrodite, goddess of love, he got hold of three wondrous apples, all of pure gold, equalling, if not surpassing, those that grew in the garden of Hesperides. No living being could see them and not desire them.

On the race course, readied for the run, Atalanta was a hundredfold more lovely than any mortal woman. But Melanion managed to keep his head. He ran as fast as a mortal man can. She drew ahead. He tossed the first of the apples across her path. She paused to pick it up, delighting in it, and then caught up with him easily.

Before she was too far ahead, he threw the second apple a little off the race course. She detoured to scoop it up quickly, overtook and passed him. The finish line was rapidly nearing.

He pitched the third apple a little harder yet. It rolled into the grass further aside from the race course than the second, which had been further off-course than the first. So great was her self-confidence, so deeply did Atalanta covet the lovely thing, she swerved to pick it up. She quickly closed upon Melanion, hair flying, white skin pinked from exertion, a smile, once again, of victory forming on her lovely lips. And it quivered and died, as Melanion, using his final grain of strength, hurled himself across the finish line one pace ahead of her. She accepted her loss gracefully, became his wife, and conceived his son.

Modern times may not have produced hunters as romantic as the mythical Atalanta and Melanion, but we do boast hunters whose exploits are the stuff of myths. Most of us are familiar with many of them, such as Davy Crockett, Daniel Boone, Teddy Roosevelt. And the hunting exploits of popular figures such as actor Clark Gable, writers Zane Grey and Ernest Hemingway, to name but three, have certainly enhanced the aura of those individuals in the public mind. But it is our loss that Colonel C.J. Jones is so little known.

Jones was born in 1844 in Tarewell County, Illinois. His father owned a farm of 160 acres bought from the government. Little Charles Jesse was the second son in a family of twelve children.

The family's lifestyle was typical of the time and place: work. It was the catchword for survival. The work day began before dawn and lasted into candlelight hours, except for the Sabbath. If food were to be cooked and a house kept warm, wood had to be cut; livestock was tended, or the plow, wagon, and buggy were without power; seed was planted and harvested; food animals were dressed out, smoked, and cured, else the stomach was empty. From cobbling the shoes to nursing the sick, it was all done right there.

The environment did not except children when they grew to the age of capability. Once, when asked about his childhood memories, Charles Jesse Jones smiled and said, "Work, work, work."

Game meat was of course an important, sometimes vital, resource, and C.J., like his peers, had his first hunting experiences early-on. He apparently had a natural proclivity that sometimes got him into trouble, as on the occasion when he sneaked away from his chores, caught a half-grown fox squirrel, and got his behind tanned for neglecting his work. However, the outcome was a turning point in his life. He sold the pet squirrel for two dollars.

Writer Henry Inman in later years compiled a book, *Buffalo Jones' Forty Years of Adventure*, published in London by S. Low. Marston and Co., 1899. He quotes Jones as saying "The buyer's offer (for the immature squirrel) almost took my breath...It was that transaction which fixed upon me the ruling passion that has adhered so closely through life. From that time until this, I have never lost an opportunity in my power to capture every wild animal that runs on legs, as well as some that creep upon their bellies."

As the quote suggests, Charlie, given the "Buffalo" soubriquet in later life, was not your ordinary hunter. He preferred the rope and snare to the gun, disdaining the danger of getting sufficiently close to the animal to rope and hog-tie it. In his day he was widely known for his exploits, which, unaccountably, are not embedded in American folklore.

He was not, however, a thrill-seeker nor an exhibitionist. The boy who discovered that the live squirrel was worth two dollars, while its carcass wouldn't have brought two-bits, became the man who knew that the value of a live cougar was in excess of a hundred dollars, while the skin wouldn't have brought ten.

It was the time when the creation of a first-class zoo meant a city had arrived. Jones had a sellers market for his live prey, supplying zoos in St. Louis, New York, and Philadelphia, as well as smaller muncipalities. He even packed bison off to London as a gift for the Prince of Wales.

In 1910 his career was highlighted by his safari to Africa where he roped and captured alive many of the species that former President Teddy Roosevelt had shot.

When he learned of Jones' exploits, the sportmanship of the talk-softly-but-carry-a-big-stick Roosevelt motivated a letter of praise to the man who had gone him one better on the African veldt.

Jones' life was not altogether a display of dizzying adventures, such as the trek he and Zane Grey made to rope mountain lions in what is now Kaibab National Forest. He knew that he was in an ideal position to further the cause of wildlife, and he did so, with monetary recompense a minor consideration as he gave lectures and sought in public appearances converts to the cause of conservation and wildlife management. He was named field commander in the conservation campaign by President Roosevelt.

He picked up the Buffalo Jones handle when he herded twenty-six of his own bison to replenish the Yellowstone herd.

Grey's *The Last of The Plainsmen* profiles Jones, and after Jones died in 1915, Grey eulogized him as a great man in those remarkable qualities common to the men who opened up the West...courage, endurance, determination, and hardihood.

Undoubtedly, were he alive today, between roping trips to the Australian outback, the African plain, the Canadian north, Jones would be stumping for a group recently formed, Hunters For The Hungry, an offspring of Putting People First which is a political action association of hunters, animal researchers, breeders, and pet and fur industry officials.

The Hunters For The Hungry program was successfully introduced in 1990 in Indiana, Kentucky, and Ohio. Meat from wild game cannot be sold legally in the United States on the theory that the regulation discourages poaching. The Hunters For The Hungry program simply makes it possible for hunters to donate portions of their kills to needy people, and indeed in many of our rural and backward areas poverty is more the rule than exception.

Officials in the three test-tube states report that in the first year the program put 160,000 pounds of venison on too-often meatless tables.

In 1991 the program was organized in South Carolina with its long deer season, where the goal was 100,000 pounds provided to shelters and food banks.

Hard-pressed directors of charitable food distribution agencies are enthusiastic. But Buffalo Jones would doubtless chomp the bit and wonder how long it will take the whole country to get with it.

Index

Index

Exotic Burgers 108

- P -

pan broiling 92

parasites
  carried by rabbits 51

Partridge Broiled 112

Partridge Casserole 112

Partridge Roasted 112

Pepper Chops 102

Pheasant With Cream 109

plains Indian
  hunting bison 121

plucking
  dry 61
  wet 61

Possum Sassafras 103

Prairie Chicken Broiled 112

Prairie Chicken Casserole 112

Prairie Chicken Roasted 112

preserving game meat 74-79

pronghorn antelope 24
  aging 73
  butchering 66

- Q -

Quail Fricassee 109

Quail Sherry 109

quartering 35

- R -

rabbit 51-53
  carrying parasites 51
  cooking 104-5
  recipes 104-5

Rabbit Carolina 104

raccoon
  cooking 105-6
  field handling of 53-56
  recipes 105-6

refrigeration 19

Roast American 97

Roast for Single and Guest 98

Roast Whole Quail 108

Roast Wild Duck 110

Roast Wild Goose 111

Roast Wild Turkey 110

roasting 92

Robin Hood Special 100

trophy 84-85
  and importance of proper field
    treatment 83
  antlers only 84
  coonskin 84
  non-mounted 86
  preserving for 86-87
  removing cape for 26
  small animal 84
  wild boar 43

tularemia
  carried by rabbits 52

Turkey on a Spit 111

Turkey Papil 110

- W -

warbles 51

weather
  and problems with field
  treatment 19
  effect on preserving
  trophies 83

whitetail deer 24

wild boar 42-44
  aging 74
  butchering 68
  cooking 102-3
  curing 76
  recipes 102-3

Wisconsin Duck 110

women
  as hunters 125

woodchuck
  cooking 107-8
  field handling of 57-58
  recipes 107-8

Woodcock Broiled 112

Woodcock Casserole 112

Woodcock Roasted 112

wounds
  effect on chemical balance
  in animal 23

- Y -

Yammy Possum 103

Yankee Chuck 107